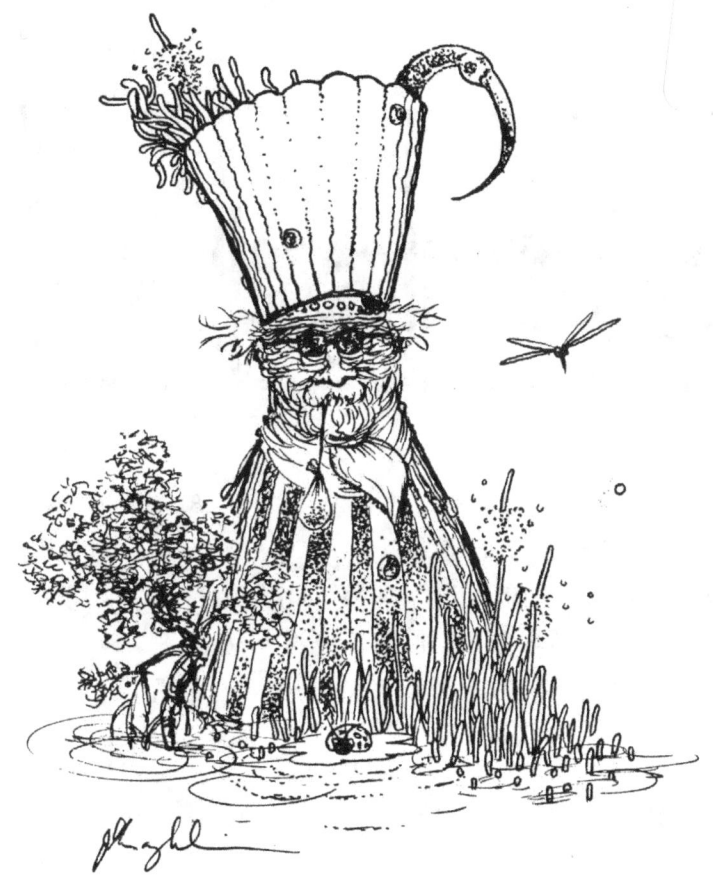

Xanthippe Dreamt of Islands

David Laughlin

ISBN-13: 978-1508977551

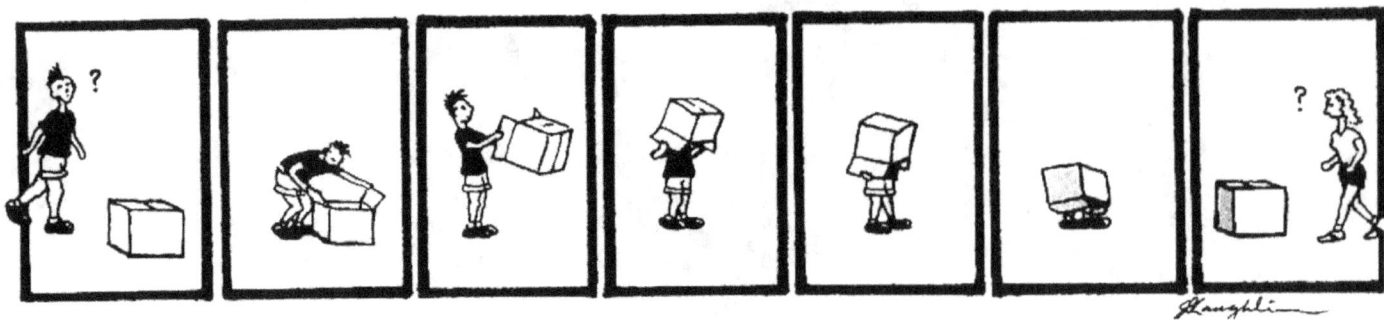

I can't remember when I started. Literally. My family says that I had been drawing before I can remember it. I do recall copying the daily syndicated comics, and, with no direction, reproducing Charlie Brown and Andy Capp in the same scale that I saw in the newspaper, because that was how I thought it was done.

Buckets of ink later — and working for others' amusement and commerce — I would take a break sometimes and try to clear my mind, open up the intergalactic channel and let the pen do whatever it wanted. Lines and dots, just to see where they would go. Cohesive images would emerge. When I felt that they were done, I could interpret them into stories, or part of a story (or even omens which I had best pay heed to). Frankly, sometimes, the final image would be nothing more than an aesthetically pleasing exercise to me, but then . . . it would be fascinating and quite often delightful to hear people relate their own narratives and insights, which I had not foreseen.

So now we come to this collection of fantasy, for lack of a better term. Most of the drawings have colorfully and successfully displayed in art shows and galleries, and I thought . . . Why not strip this work down to the original black-and-white format, and present them for you to play with, too?

Why not, indeed?

Let your imagination loose, add your own color, create your own stories. Take it from here.

I hope that you enjoy my creations. Whatever they will be for you.

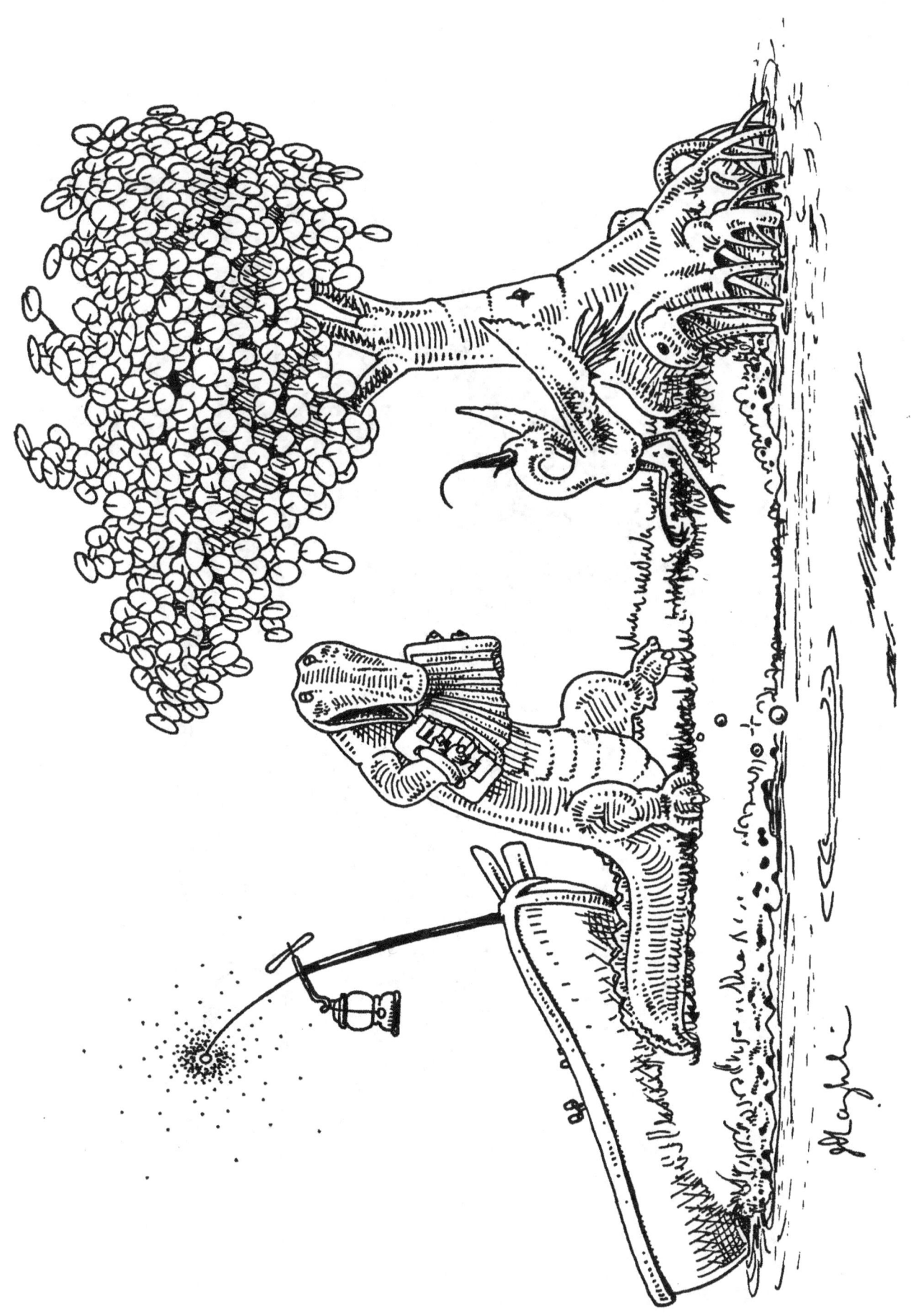

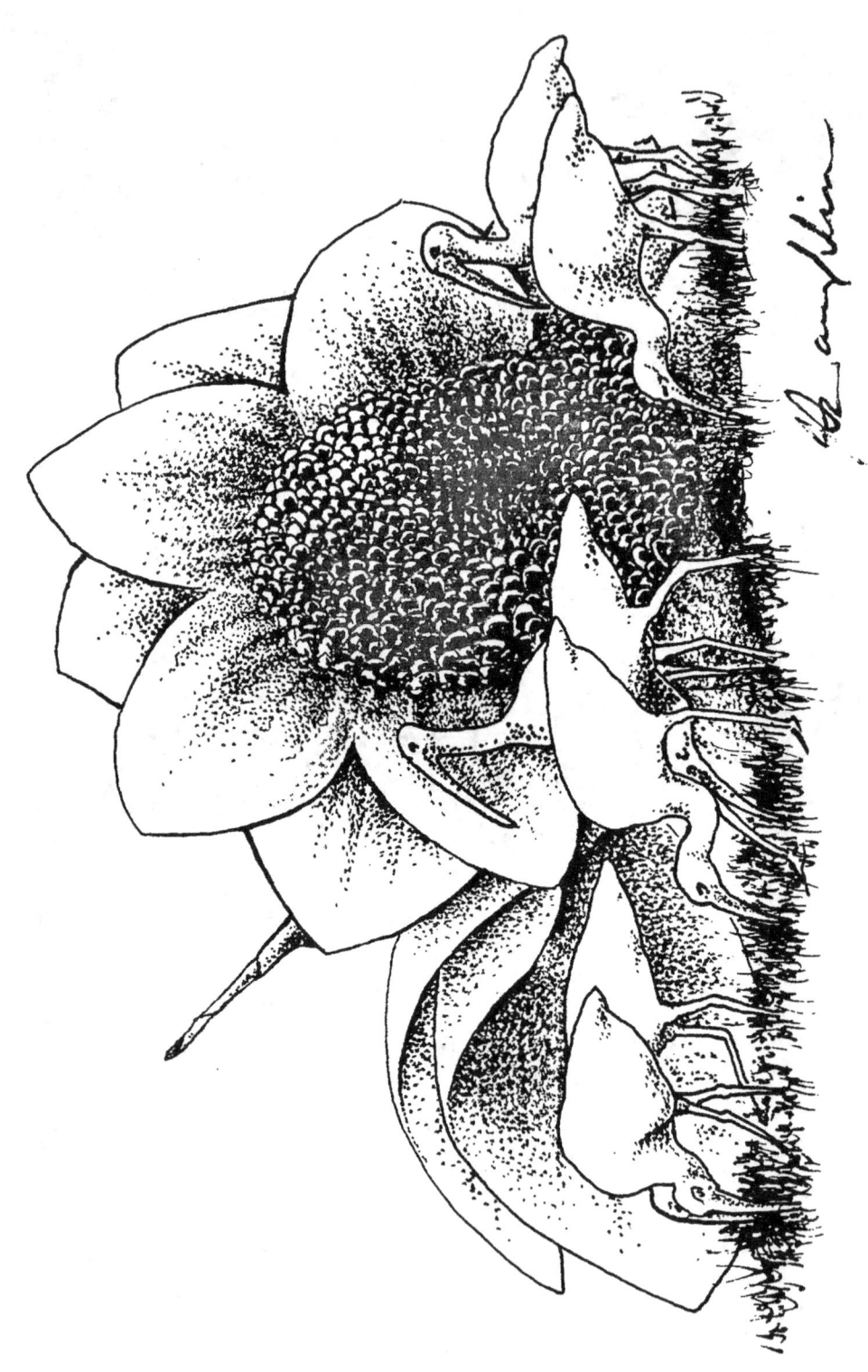

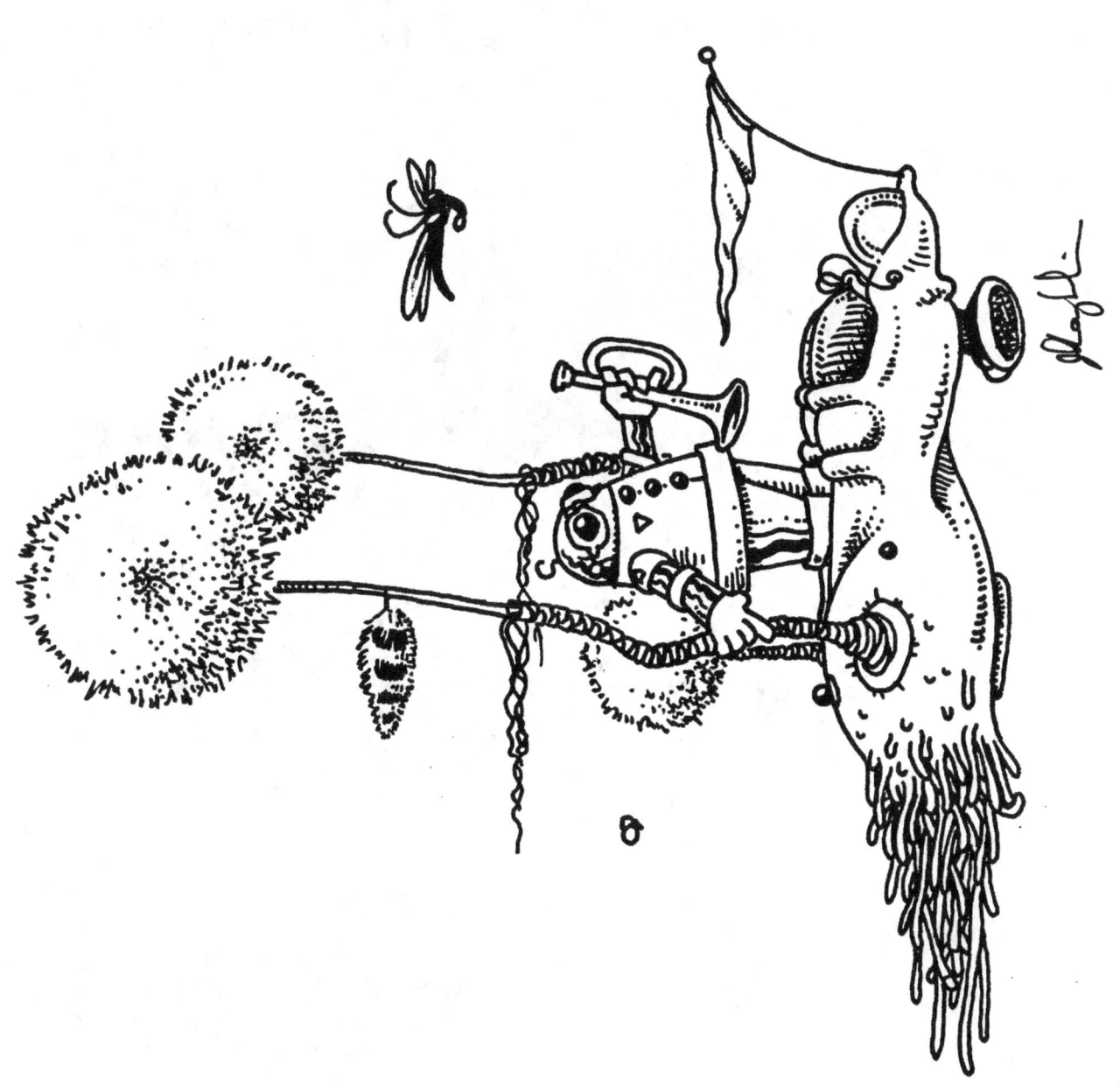

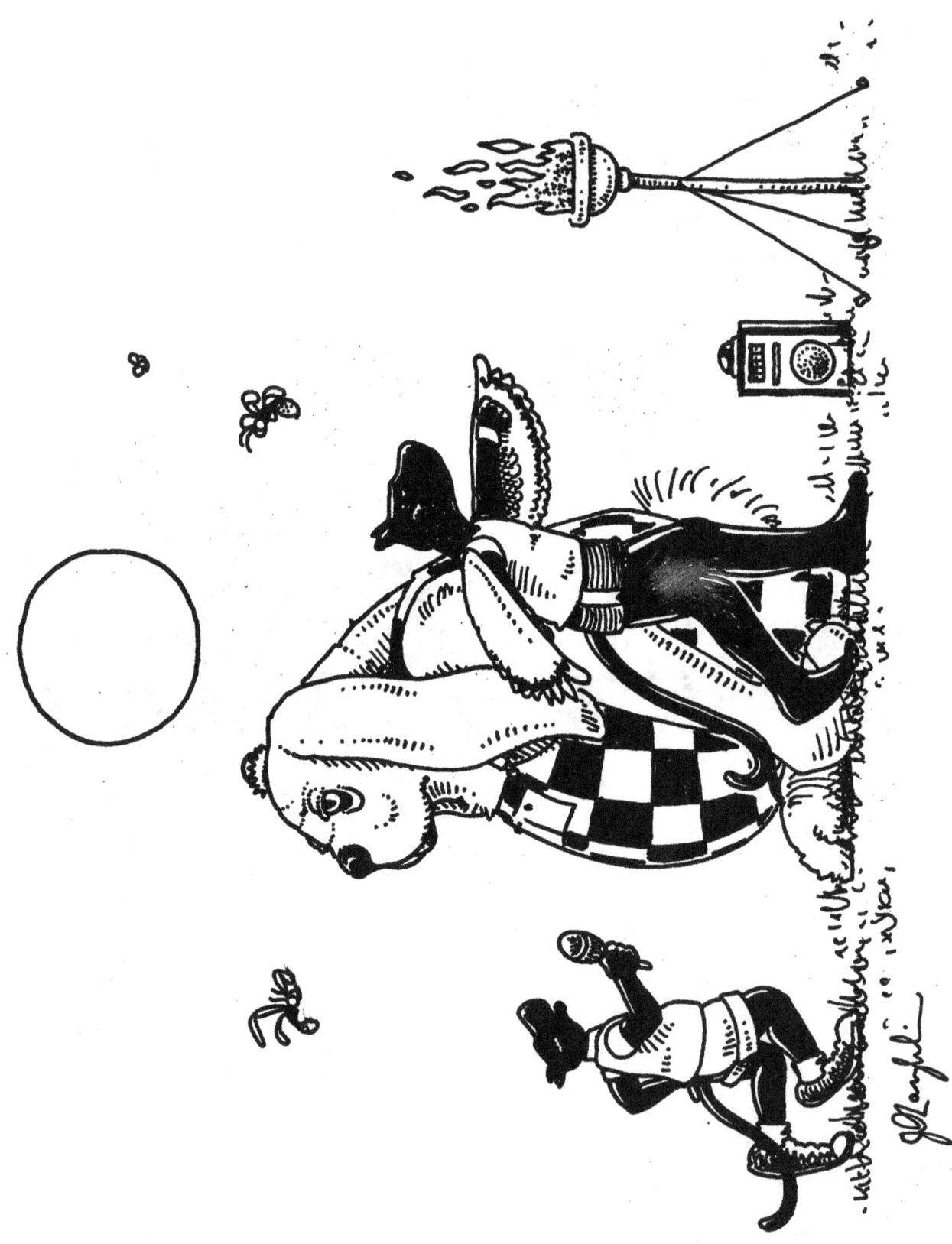

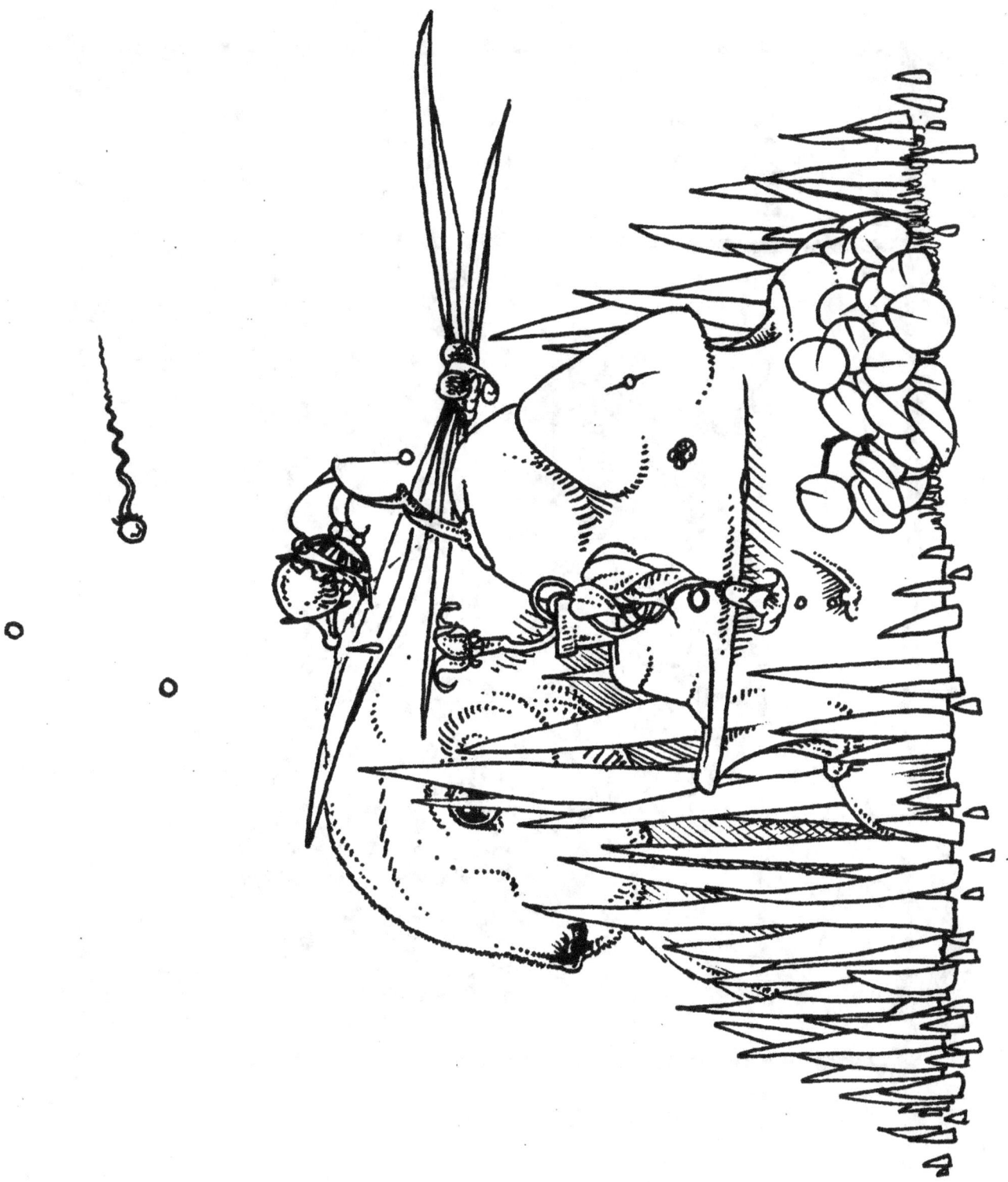

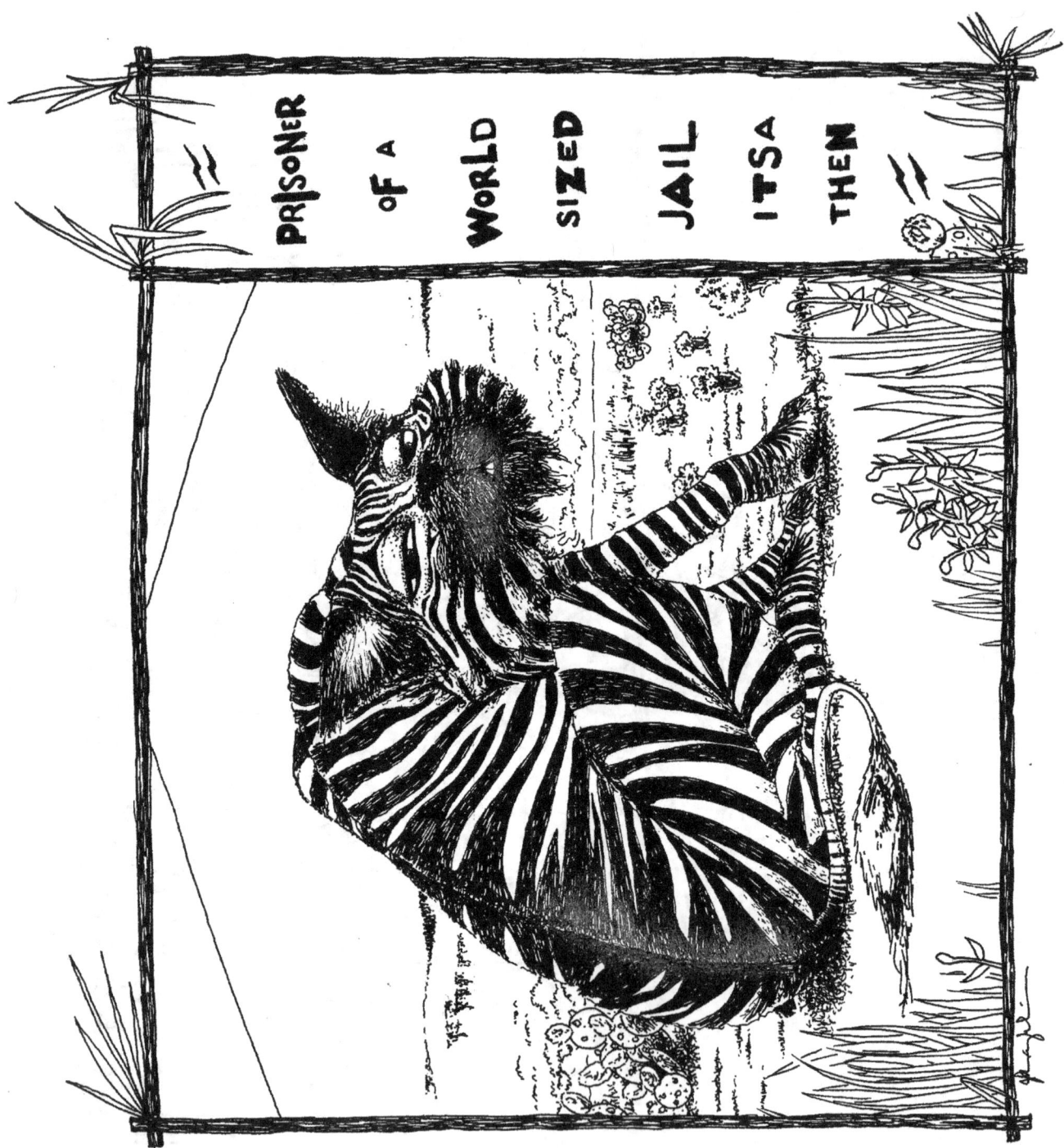

PRISONER OF A WORLD SIZED JAIL ITSA THEN

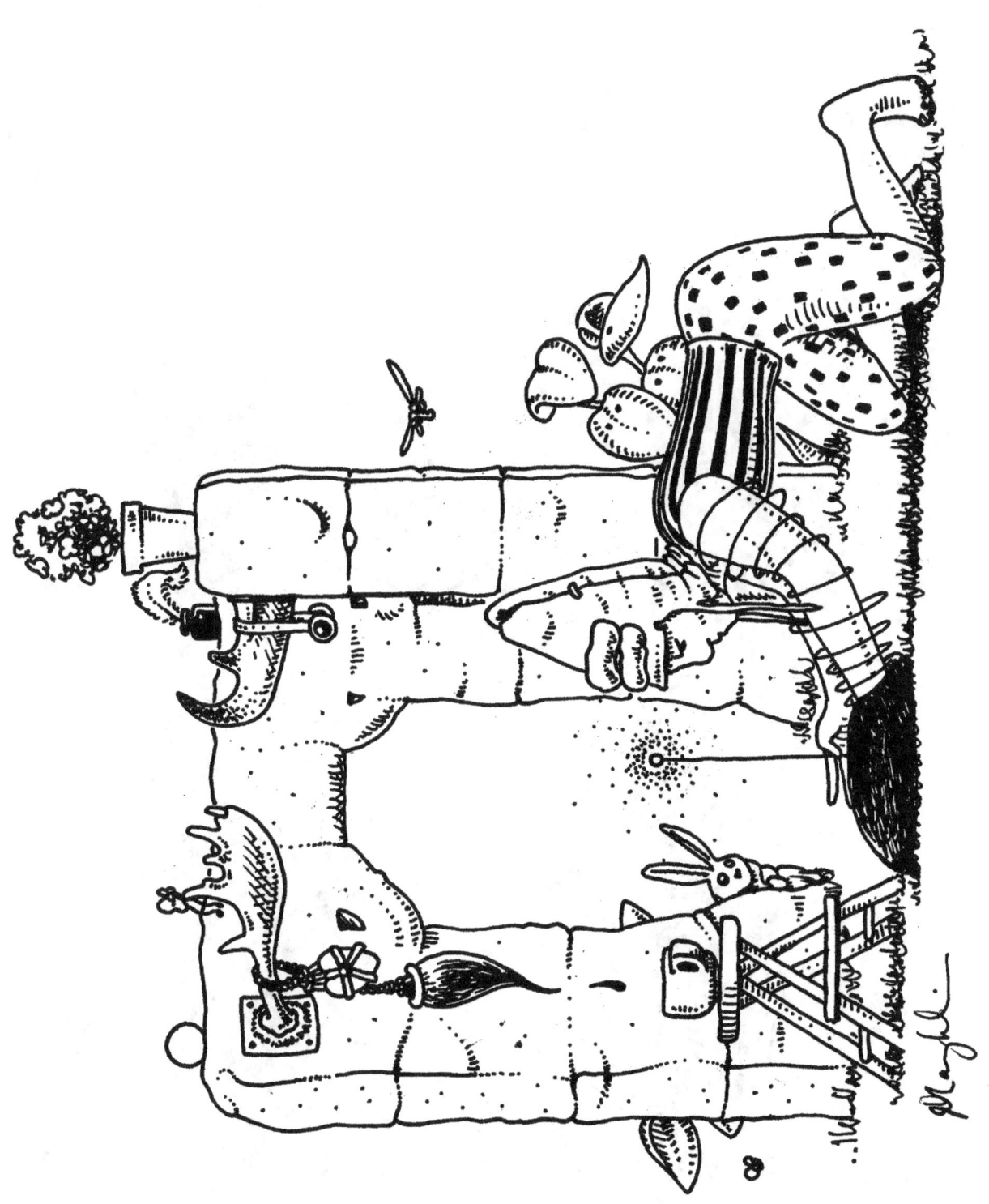

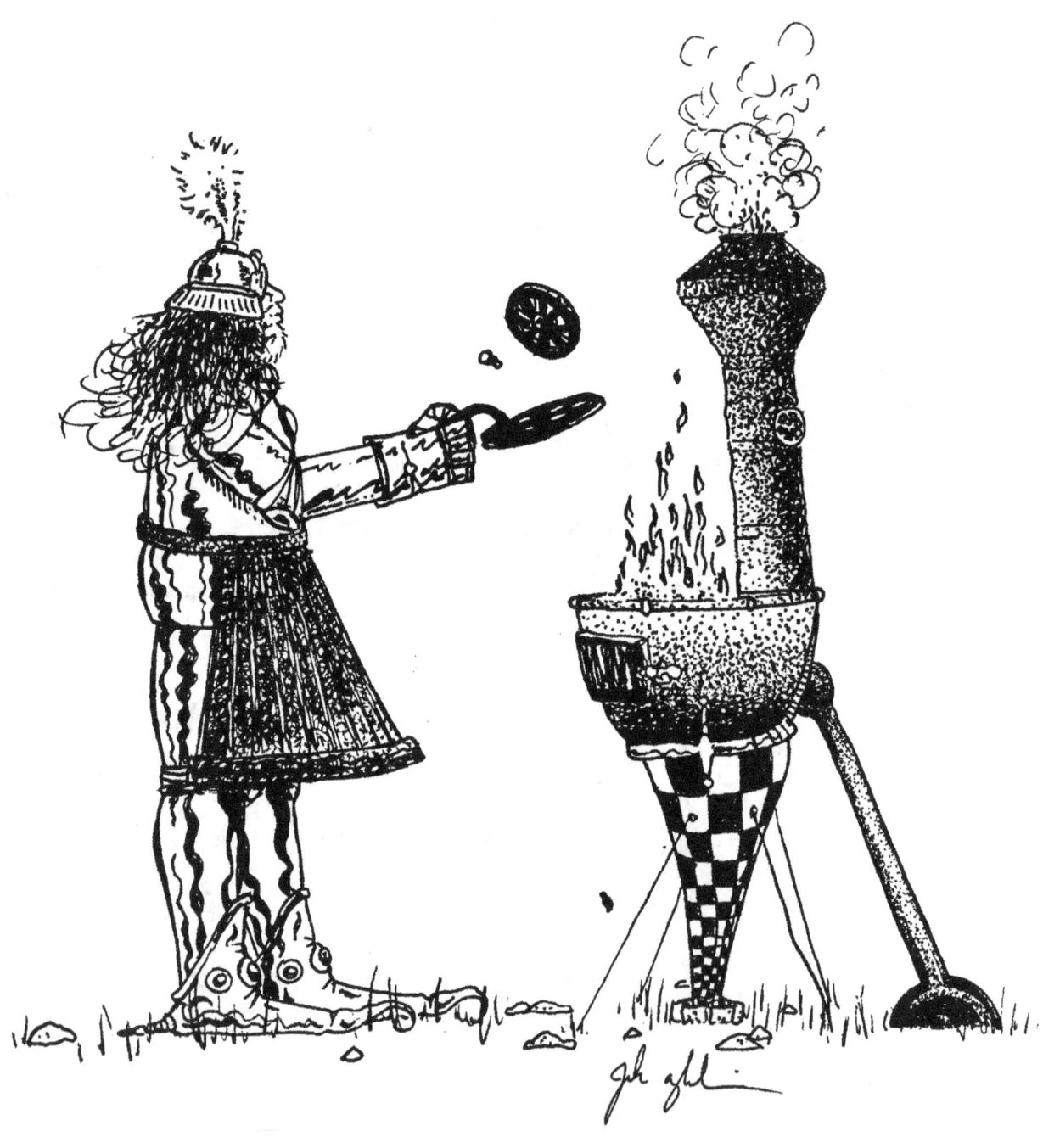

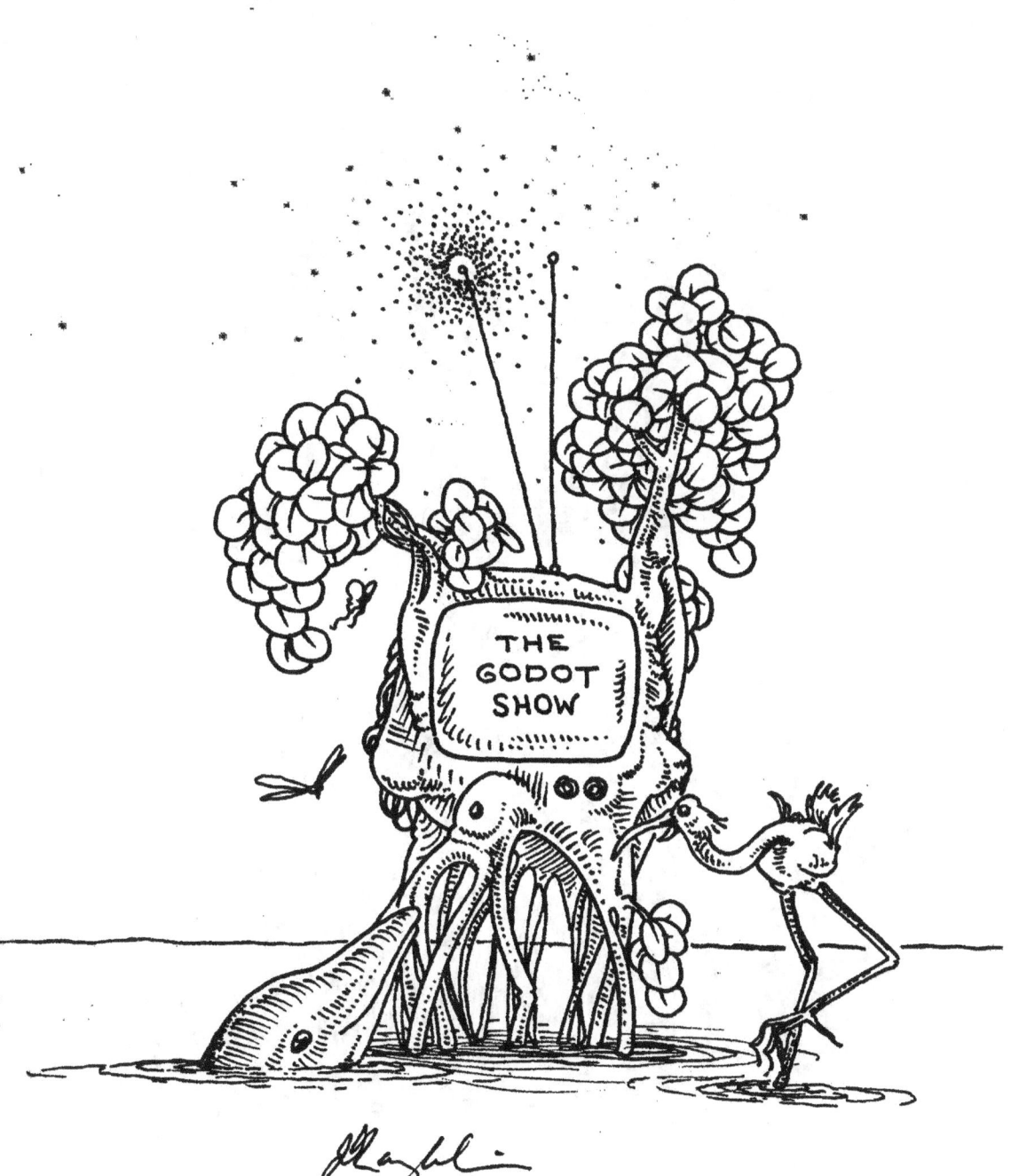

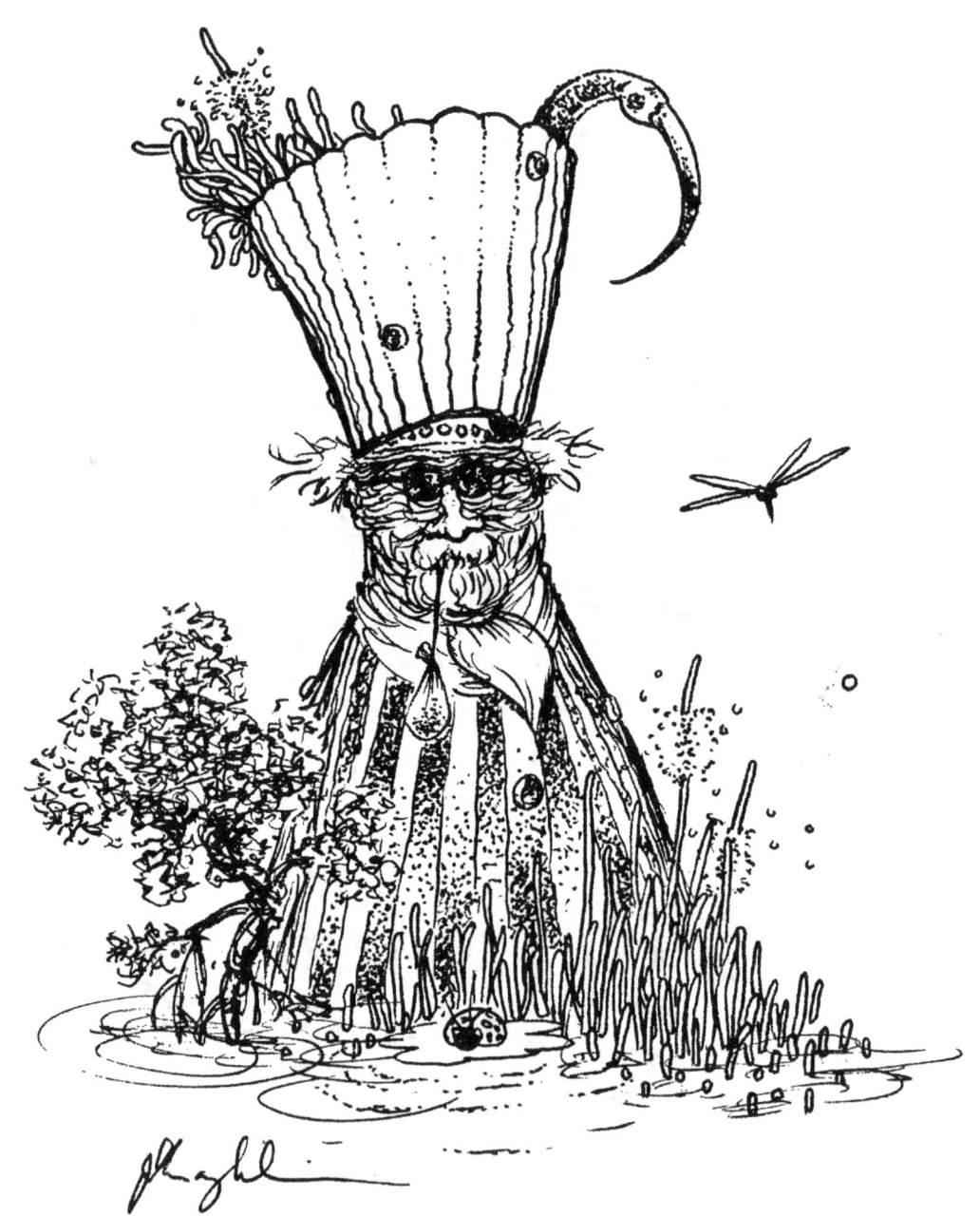

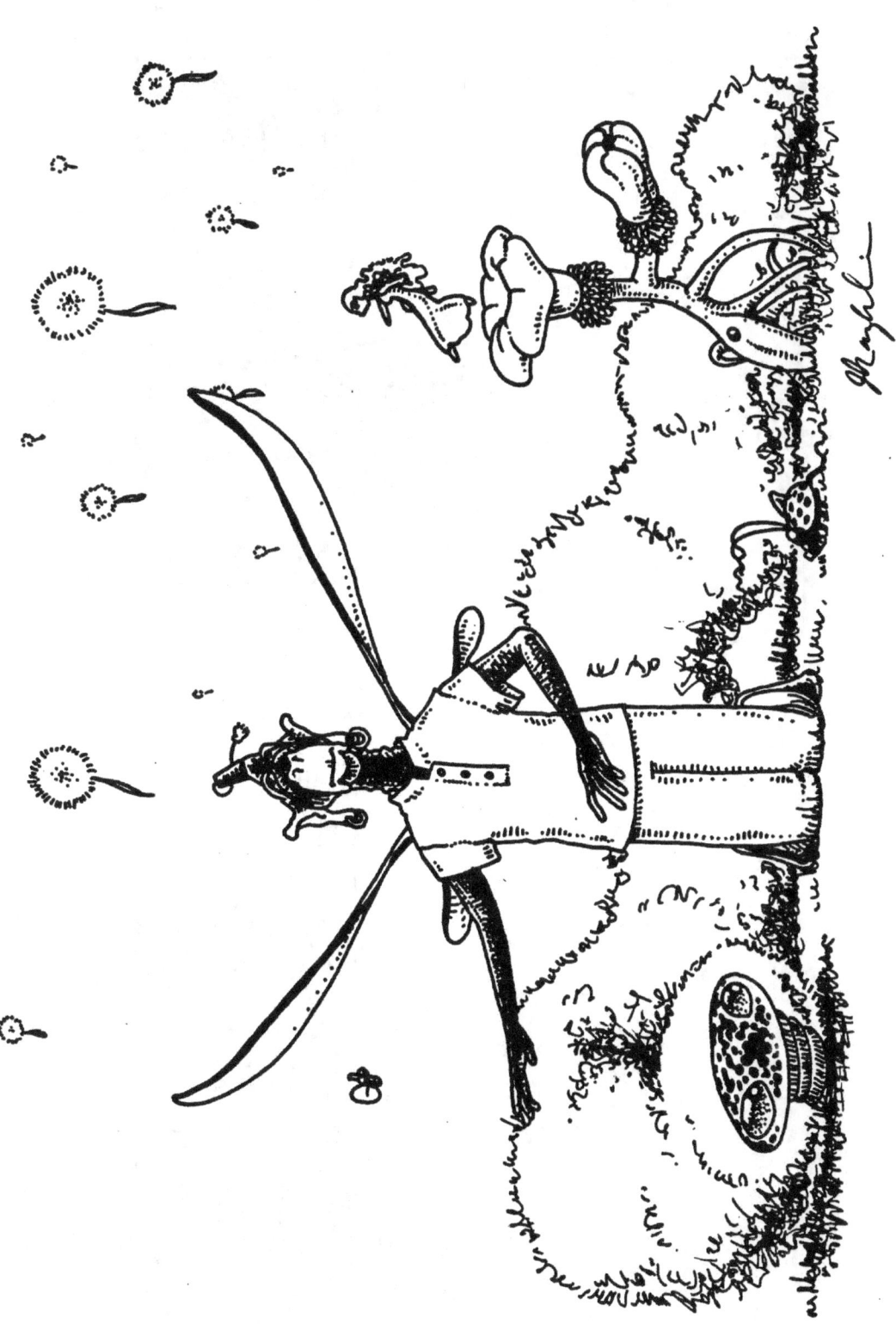

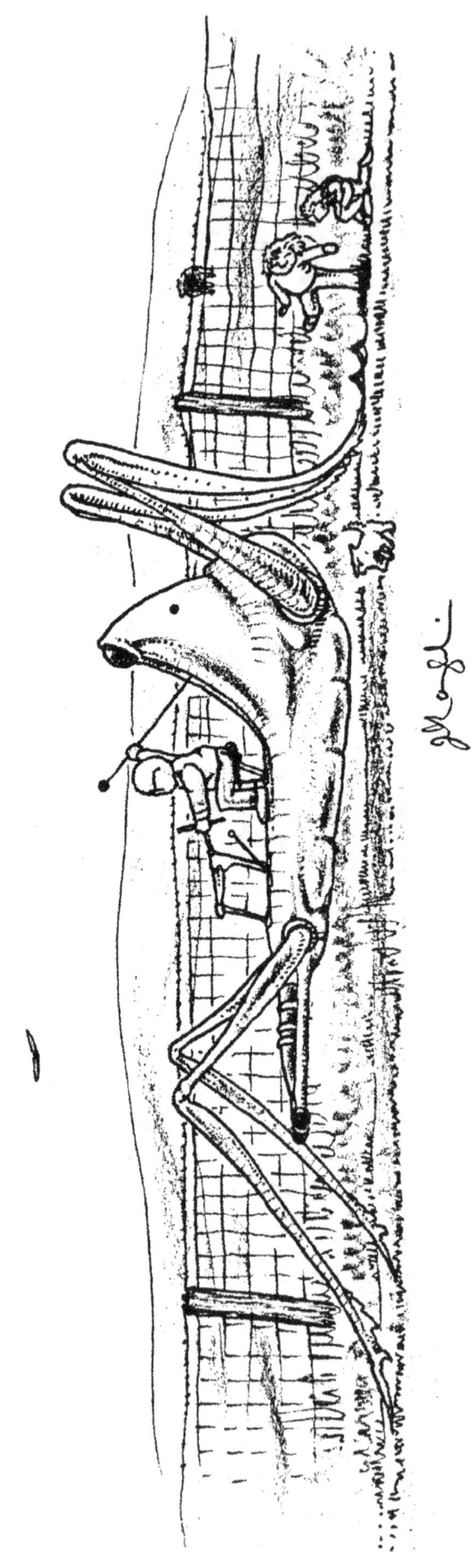

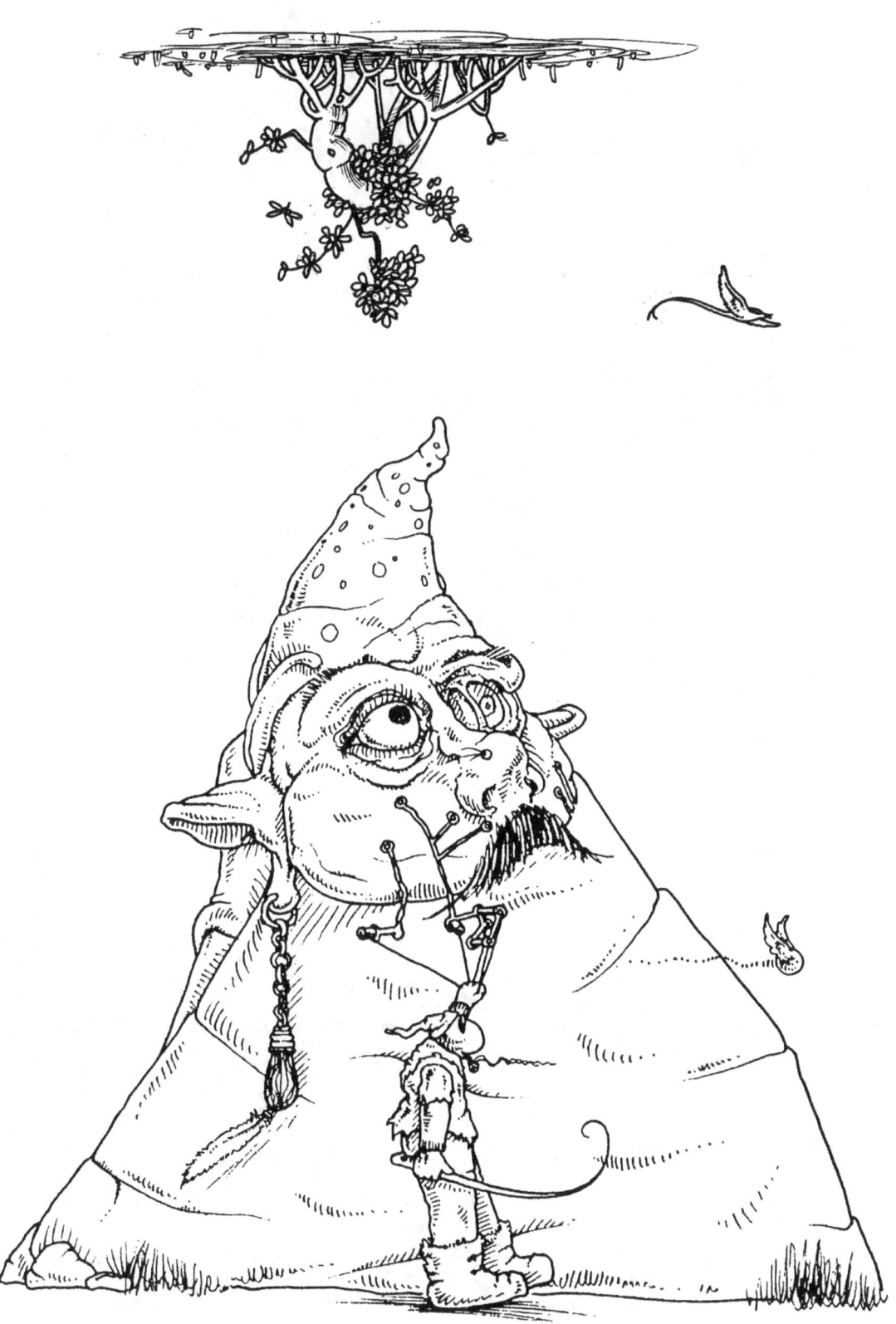

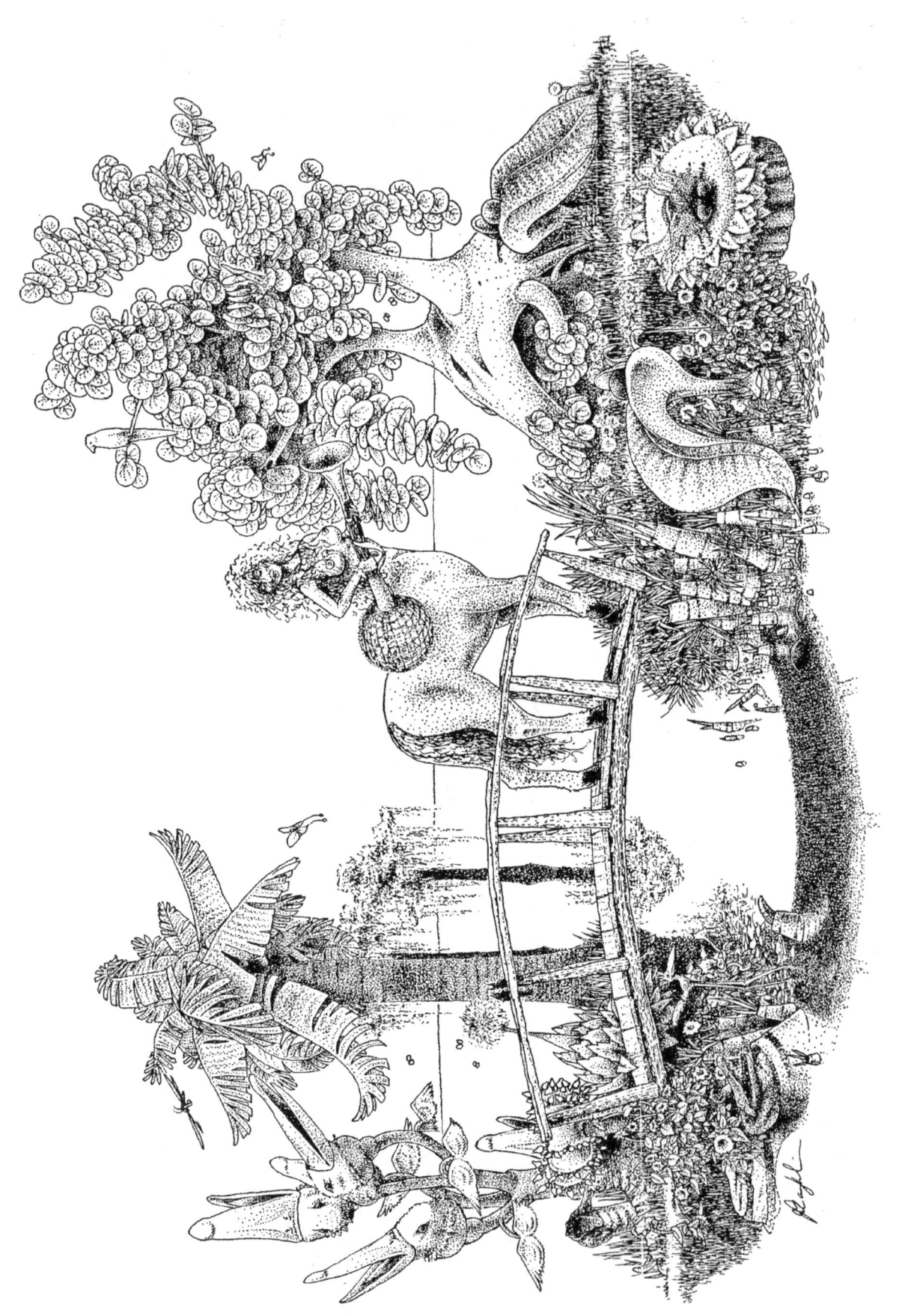

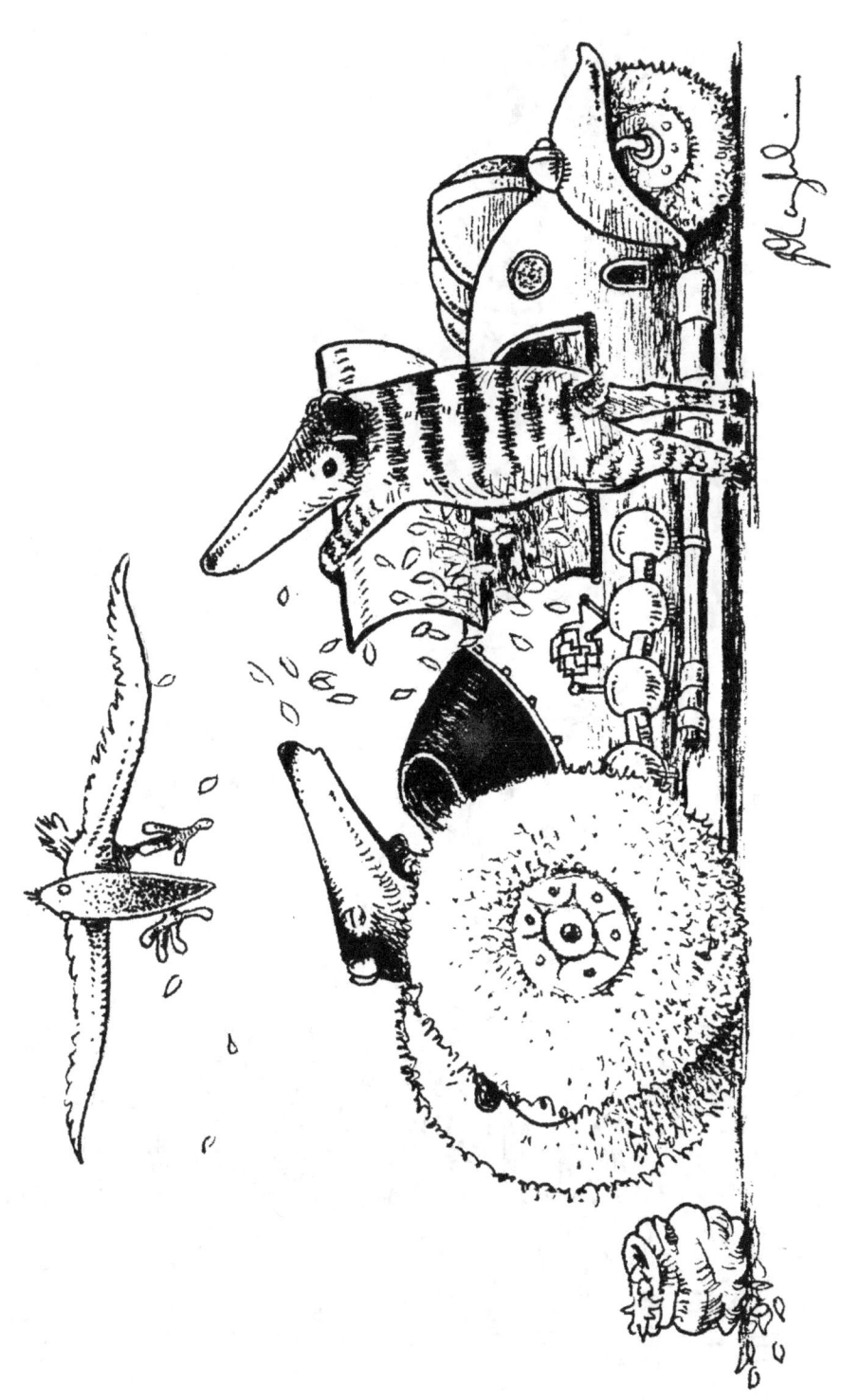

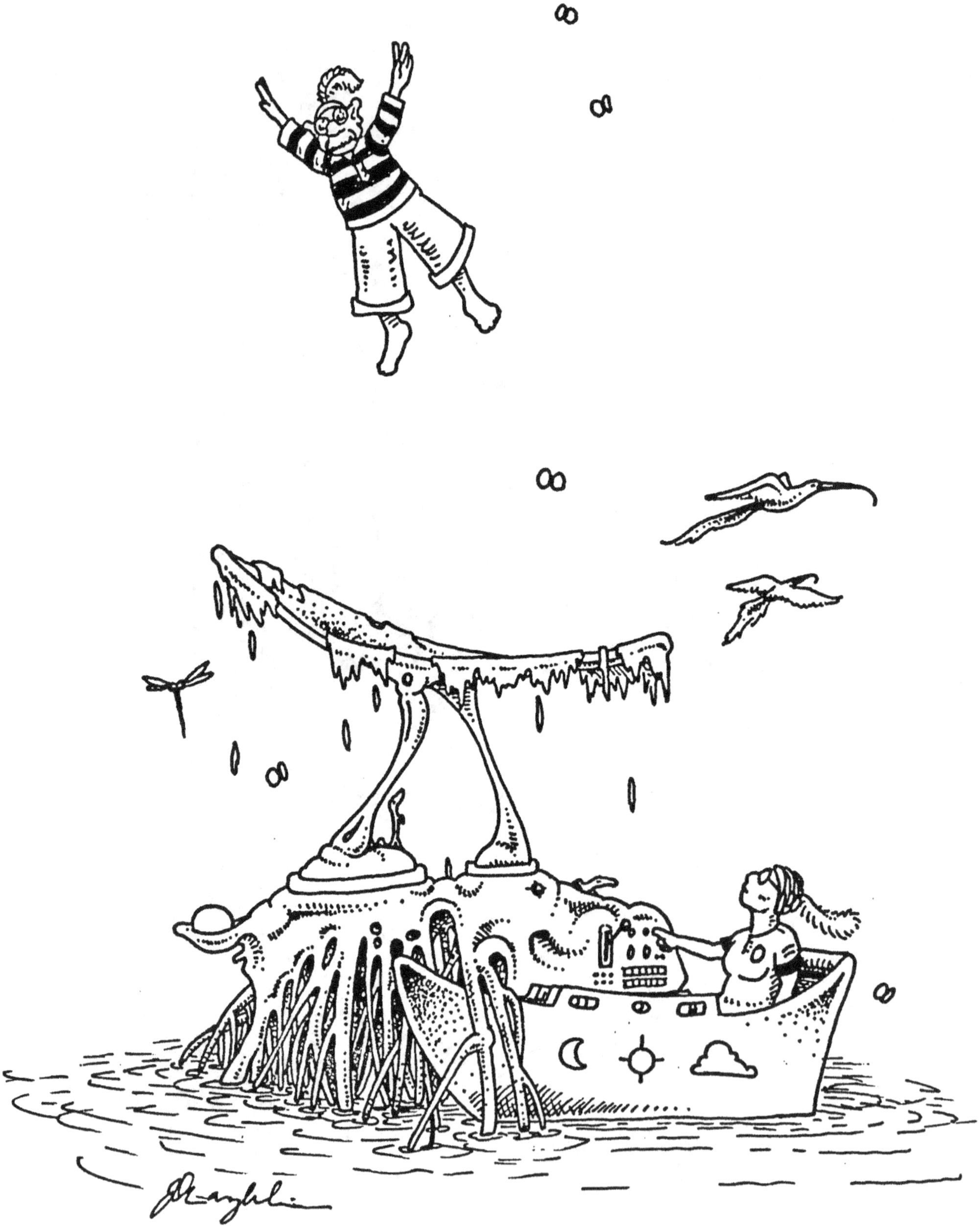

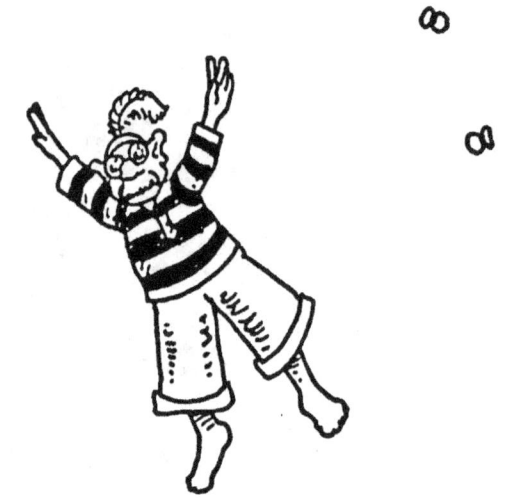

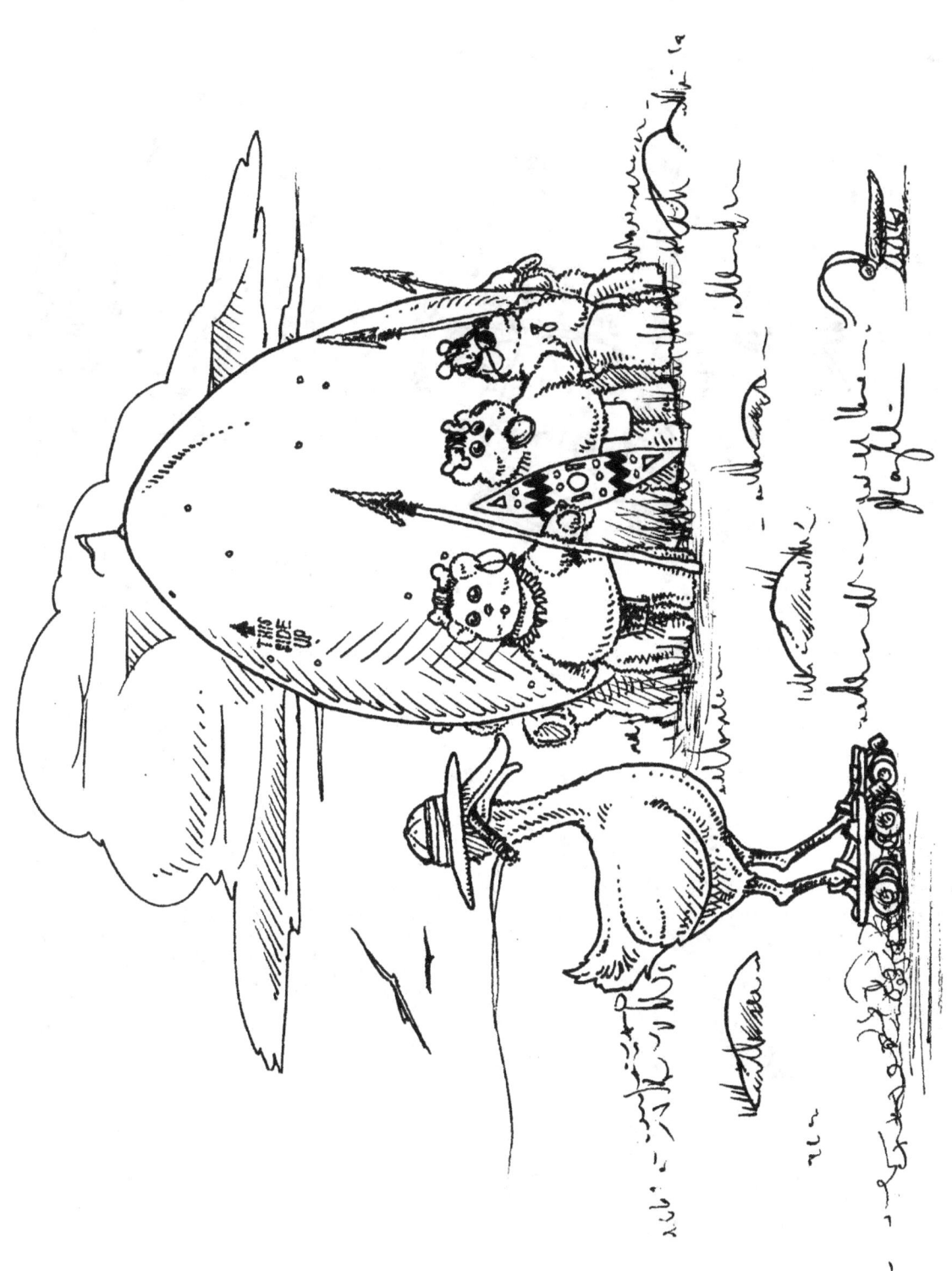

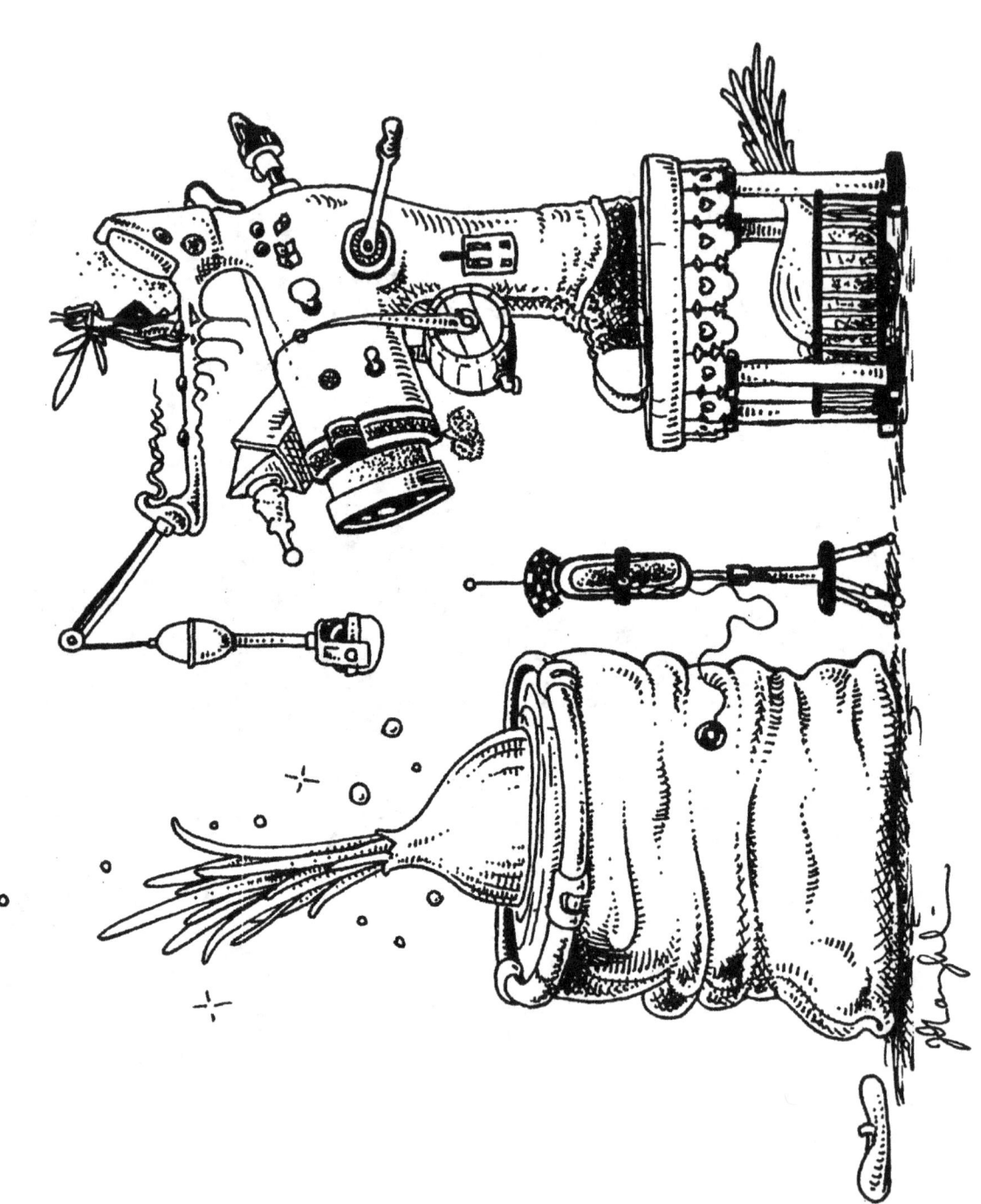

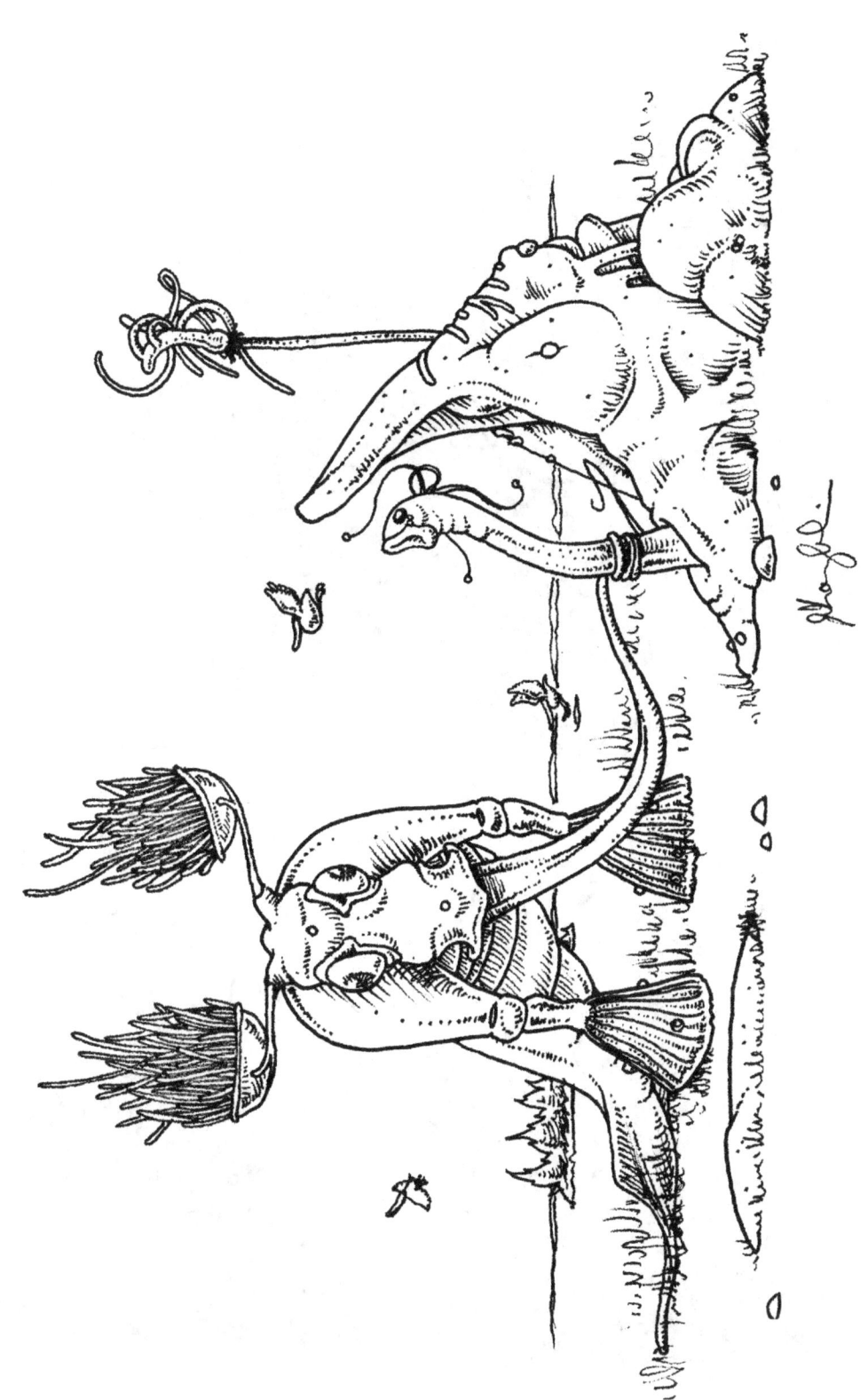

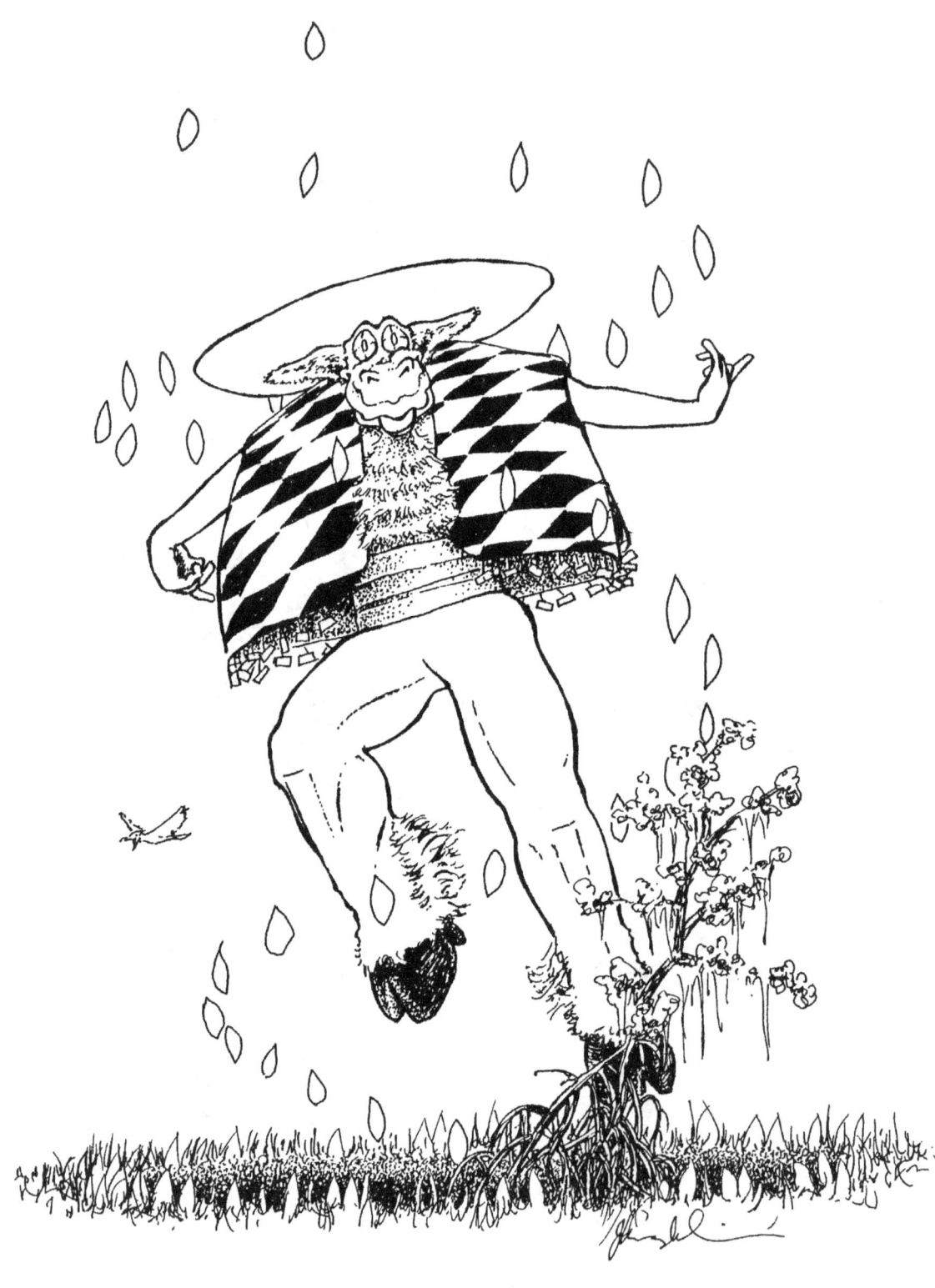

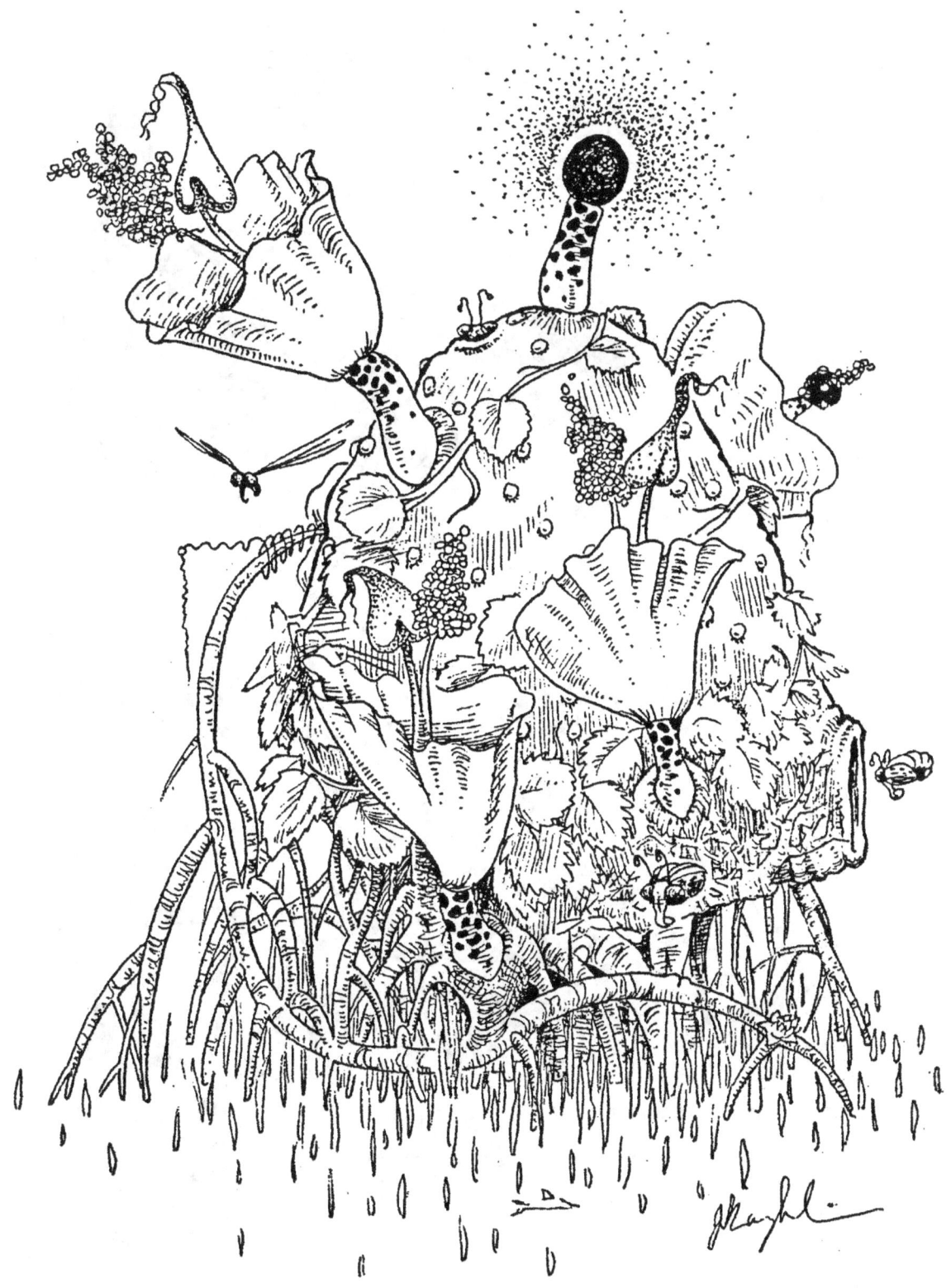

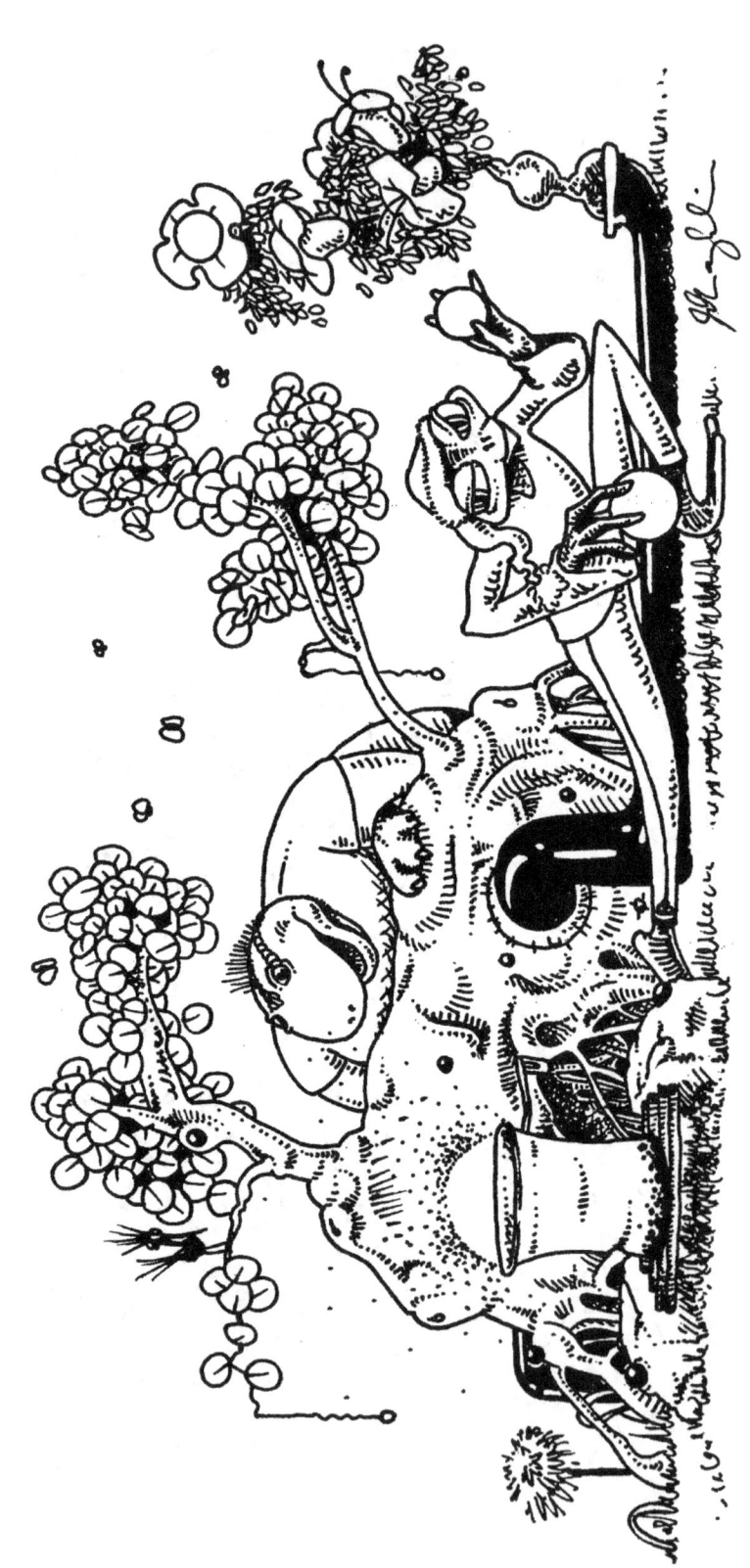

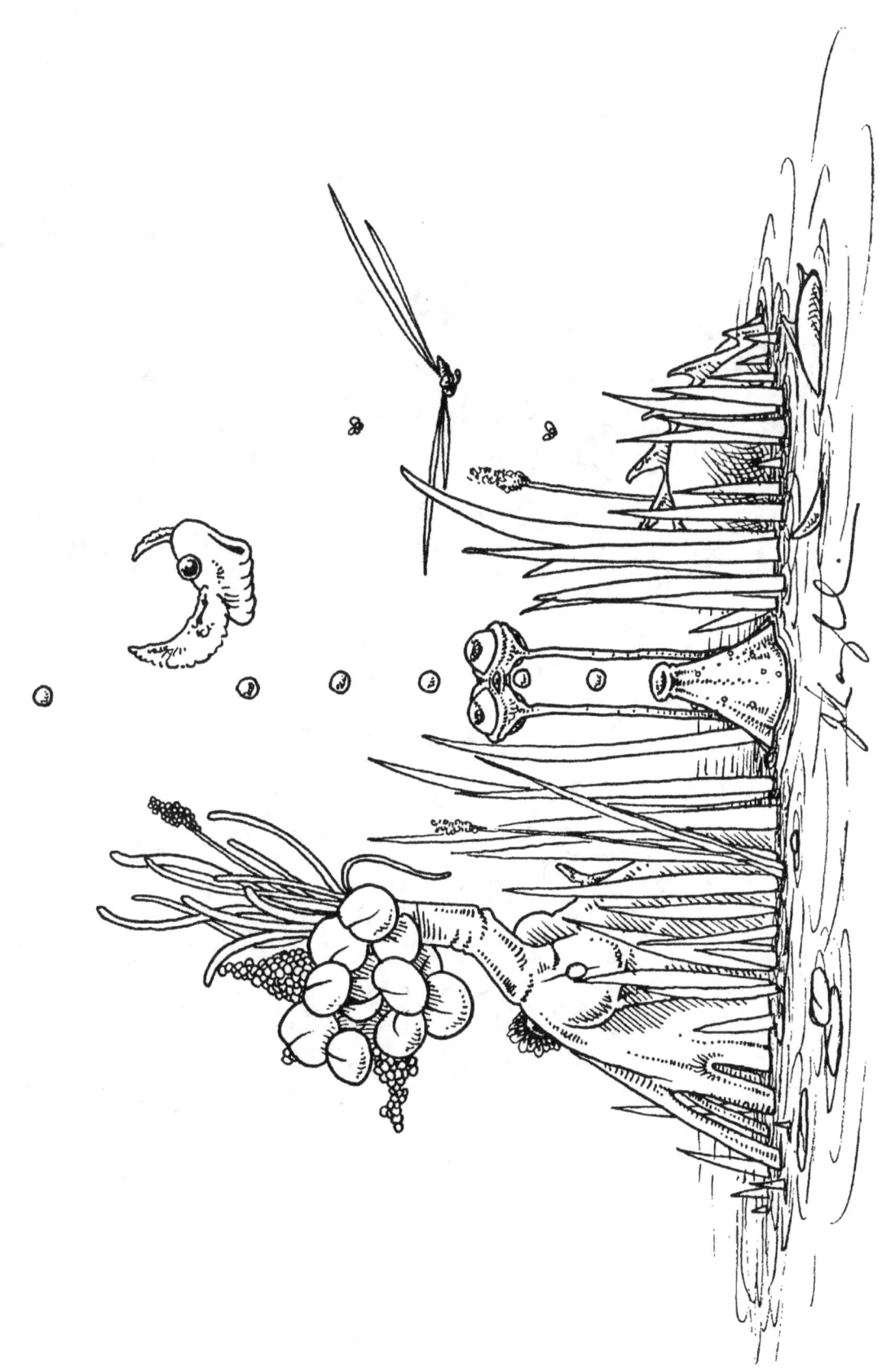

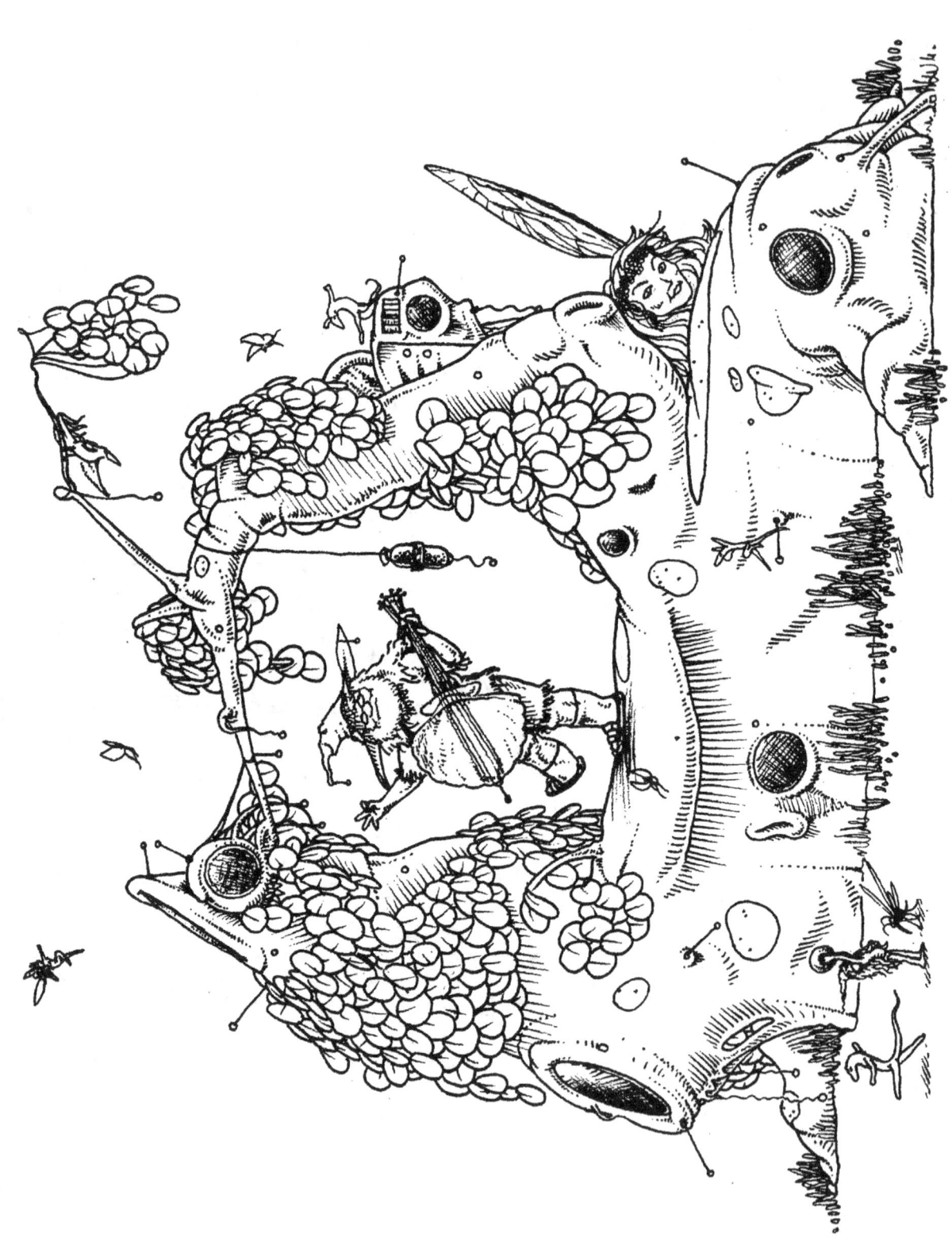

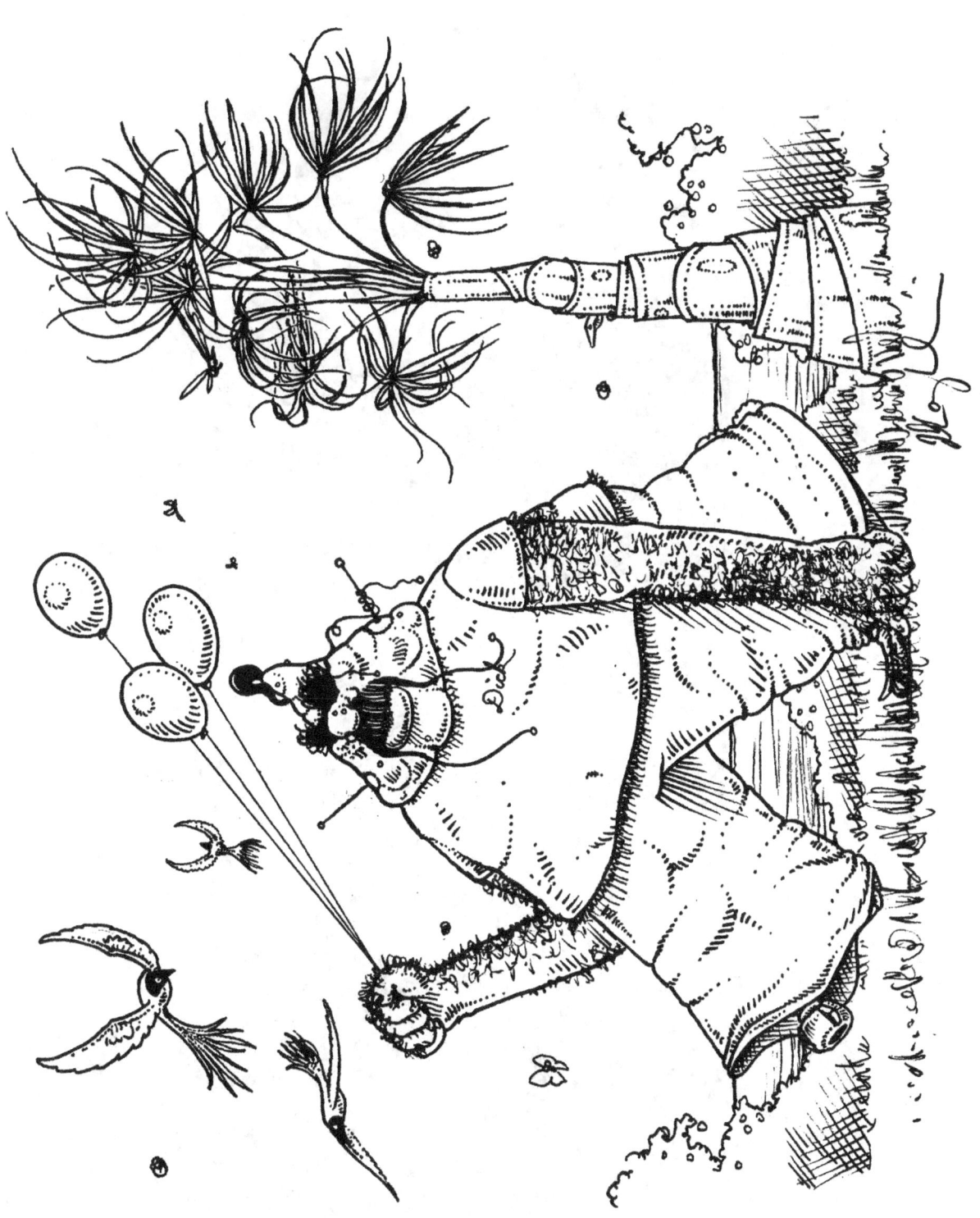

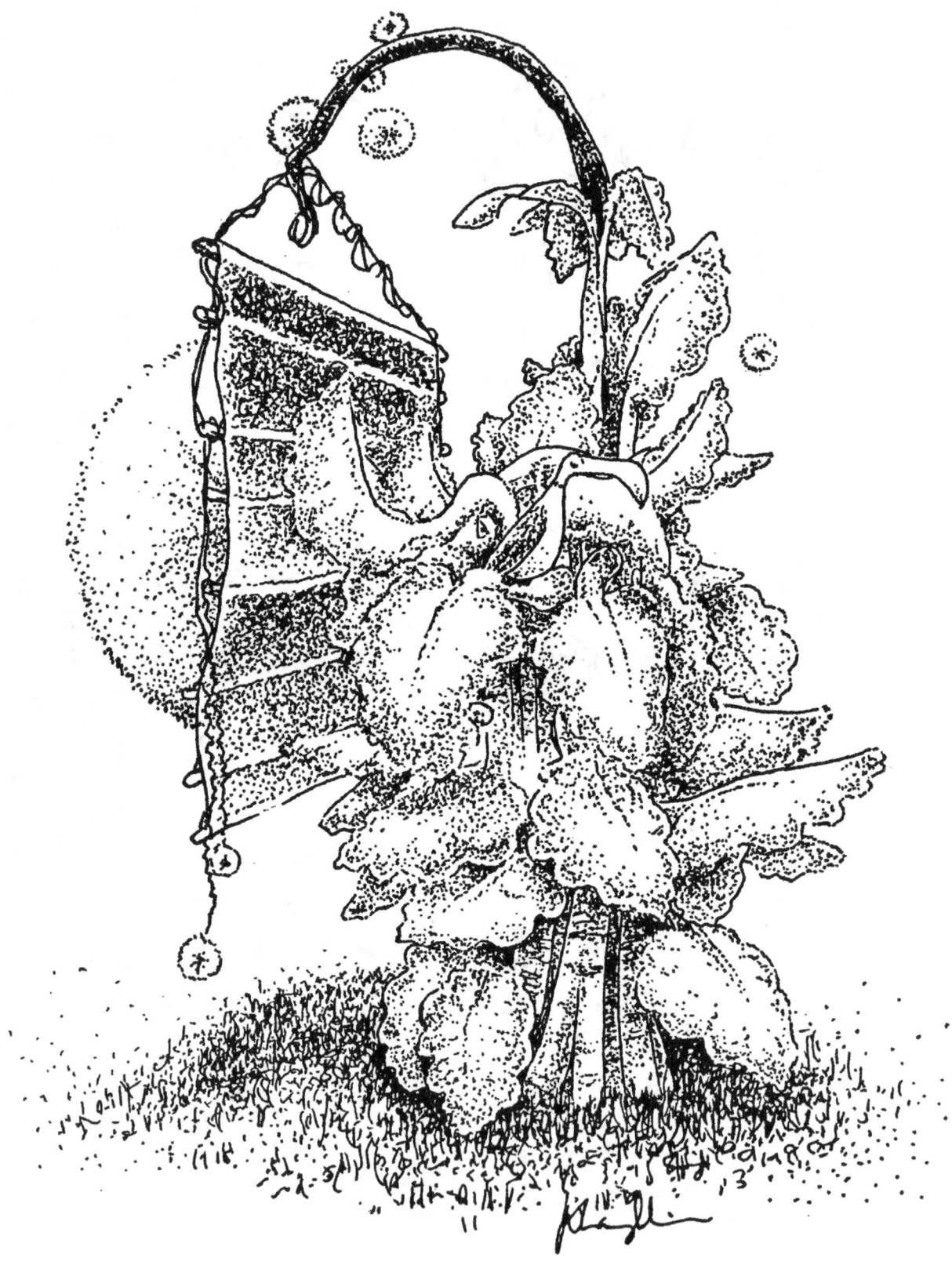

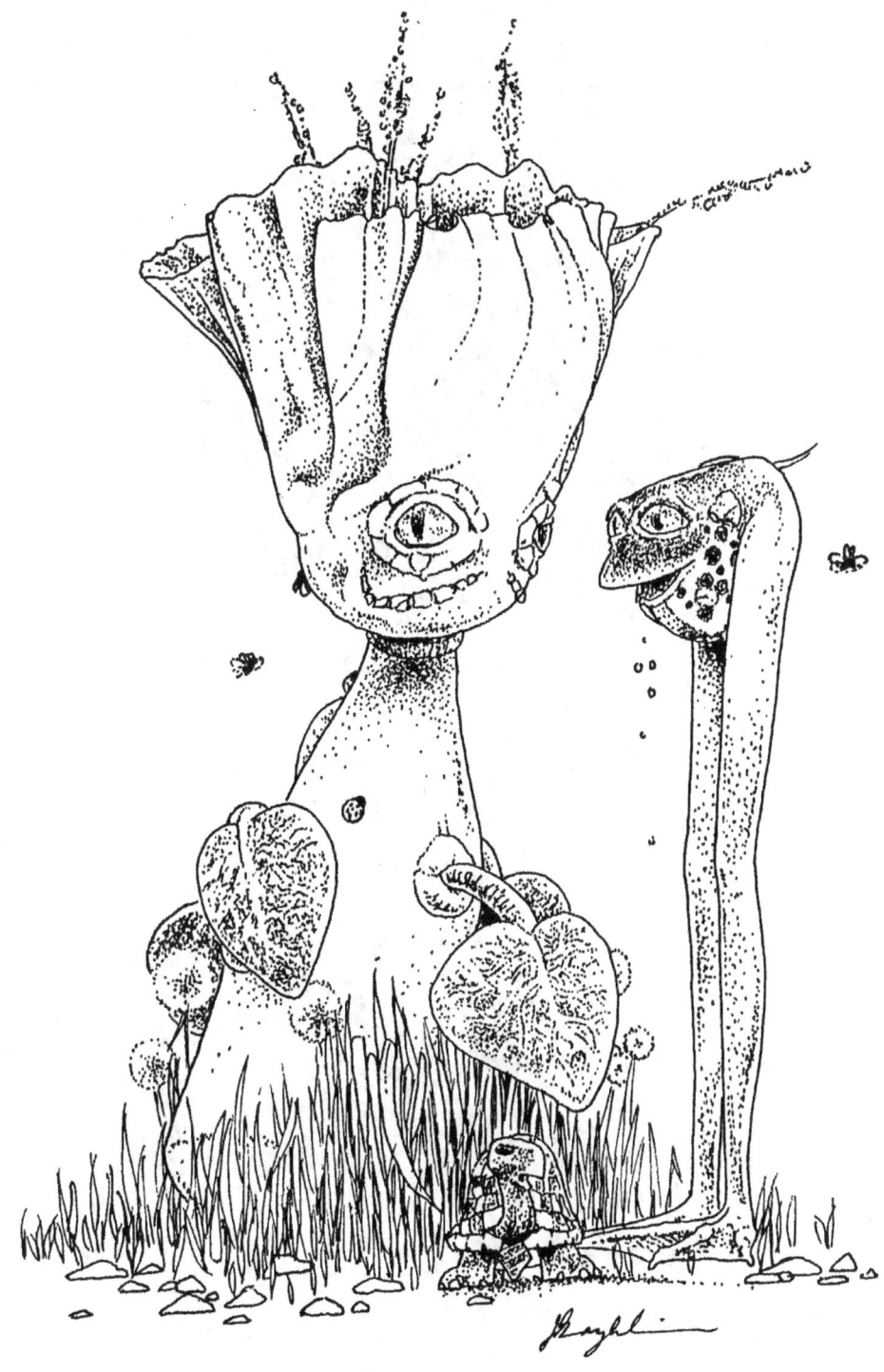

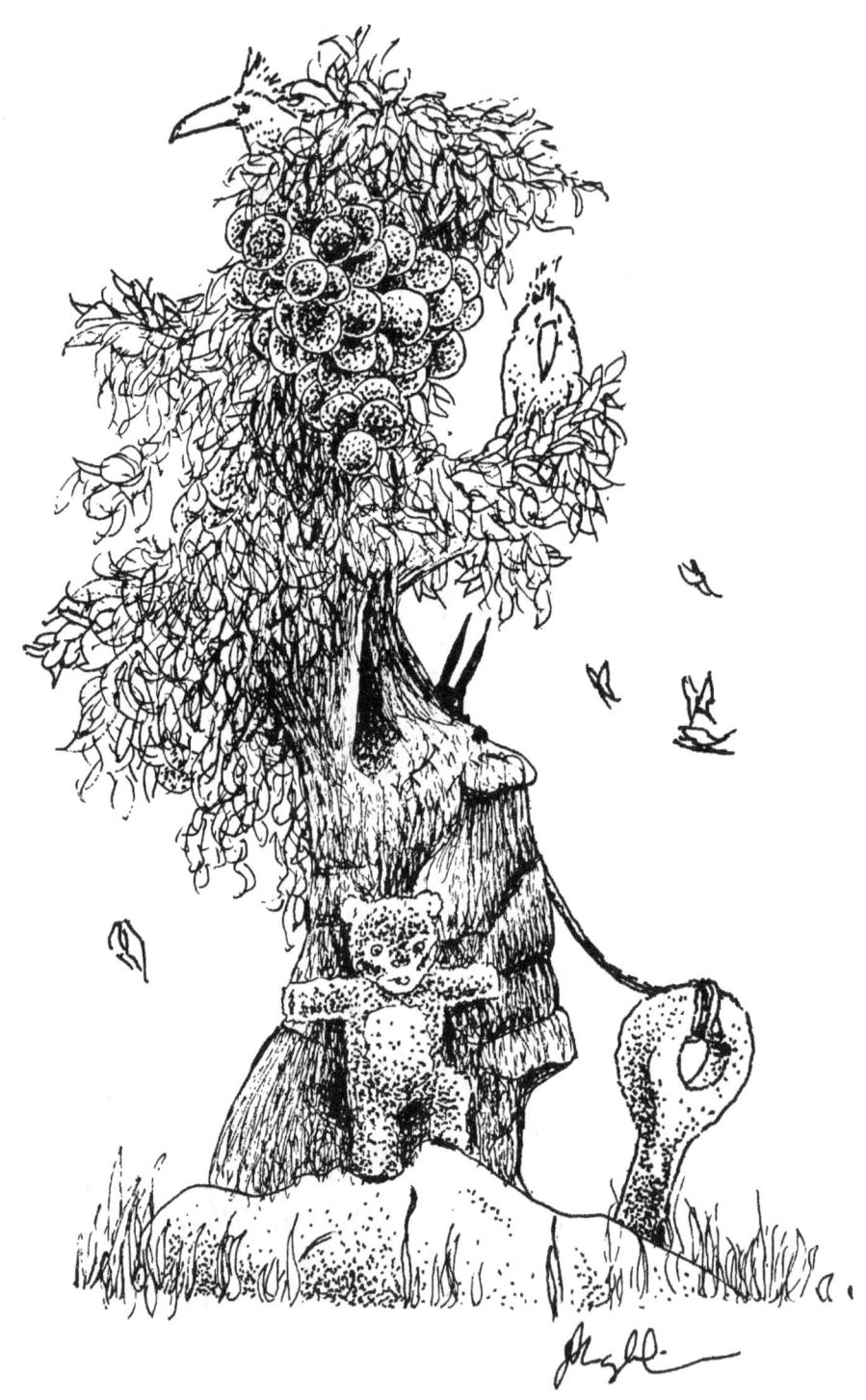

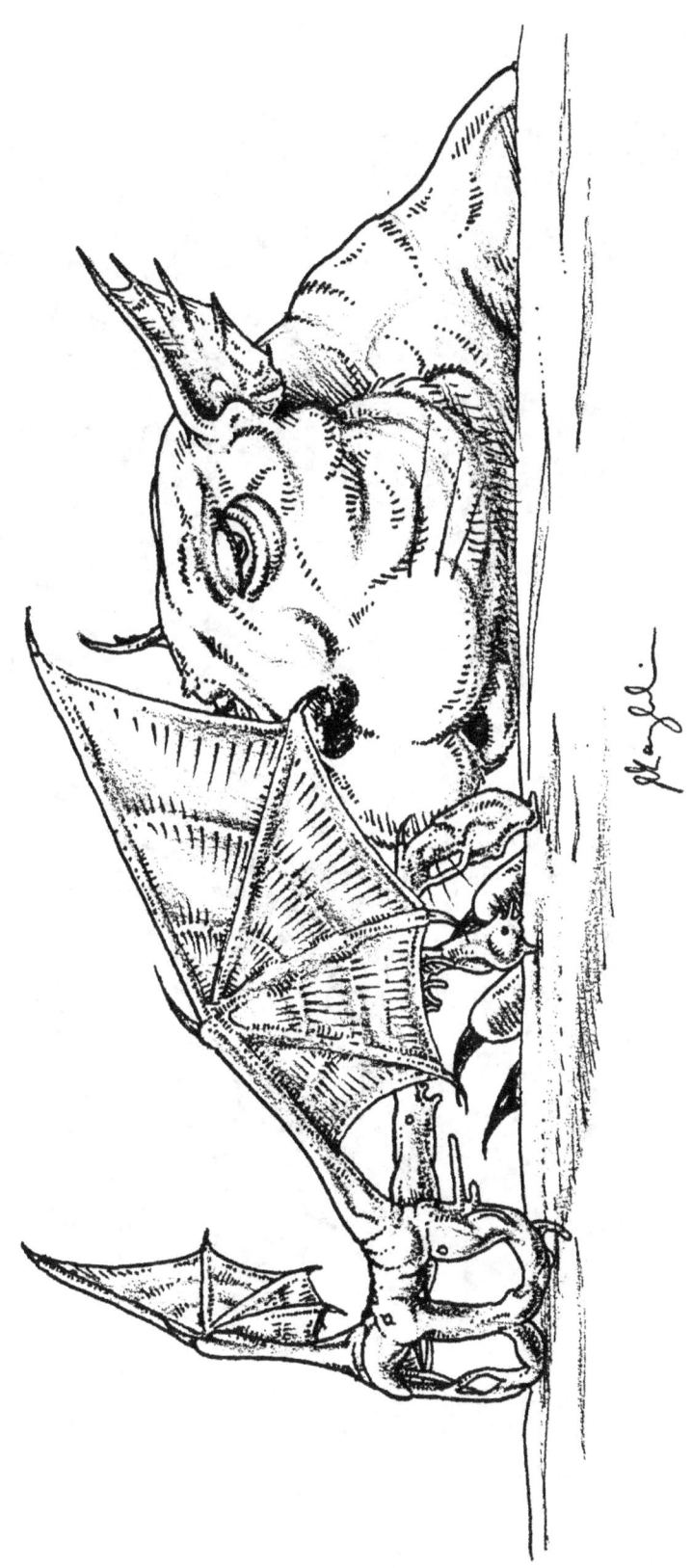

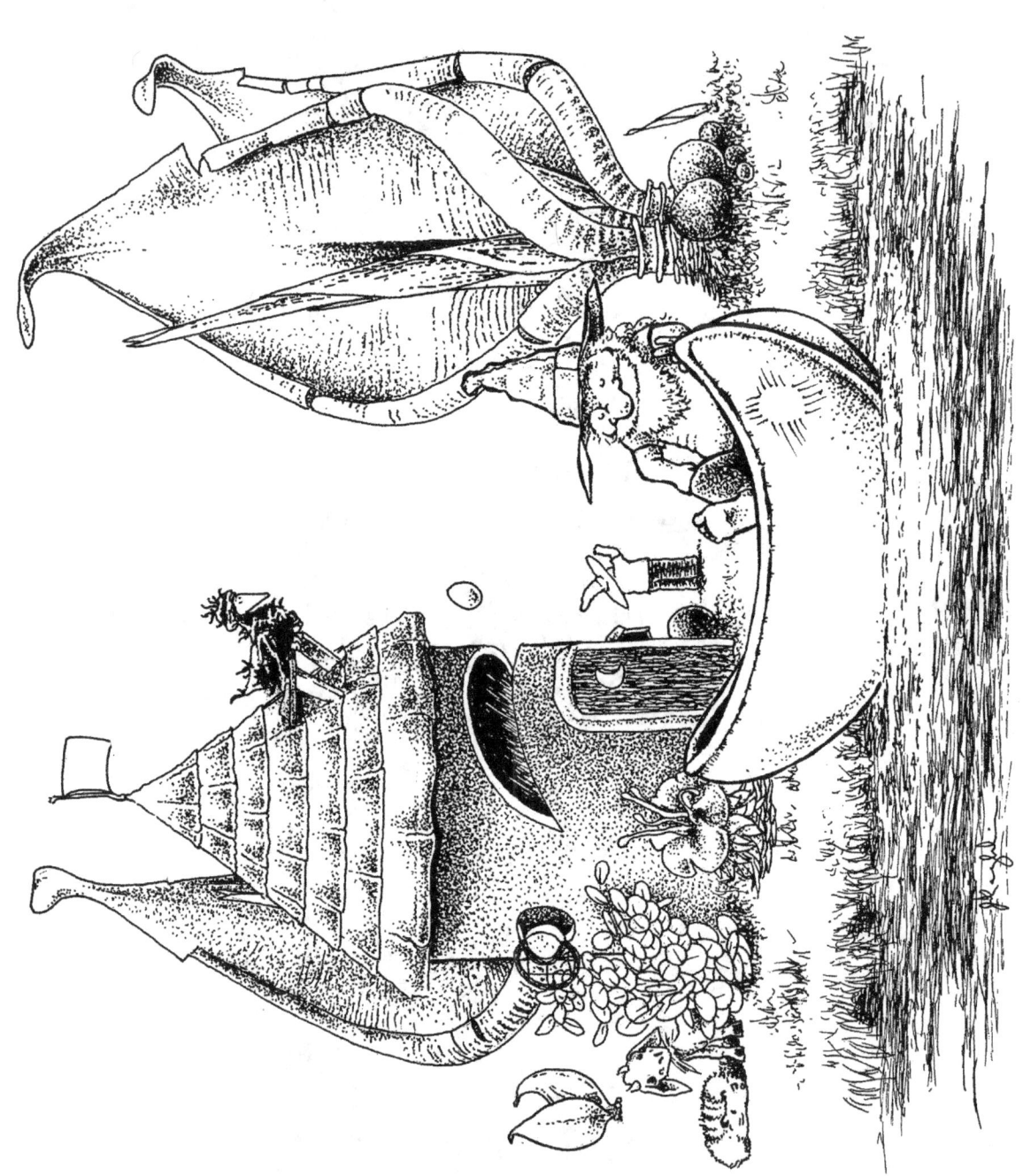

www.ingramcontent.com/pod-product-compliance
Lightning Source LLC
Chambersburg PA
CBHW082305200526
45168CB00018B/3411